AGHT'AMAR

CHURCH OF THE HOLY CROSS

BY SIRARPIE DER NERSESSIAN

HARVARD UNIVERSITY PRESS · CAMBRIDGE, MASSACHUSETTS · 1965

DISTRIBUTED IN GREAT BRITAIN BY OXFORD UNIVERSITY PRESS, LONDON

PUBLICATION OF THIS BOOK HAS BEEN AIDED BY GRANTS FROM THE ARMENIAN FUNDS
OF HARVARD UNIVERSITY, FROM DUMBARTON OAKS, TRUSTEES FOR HARVARD UNIVERSITY,
AND FROM THE FORD FOUNDATION

LIBRARY OF CONGRESS CATALOG CARD NUMBER 64-21241

PRINTED IN THE UNITED STATES OF AMERICA

FOREWORD

THE present volume on the Armenian Church of Aght'amar launches the Harvard Armenian Texts and Studies series of the Department of Near Eastern Languages and Literatures.

Sirarpie Der Nersessian, Henri Focillon Professor of Byzantine Art and Archaeology, Emerita, at Dumbarton Oaks, Washington, D.C., is an eminent scholar in the areas of both Byzantine and Armenian art who requires no introduction. Her numerous scholarly contributions to these fields—be they in her published works of unusual beauty and clarity, or her spoken lectures and presentations of exquisite charm and delicate authority—are testimony to her vast erudition and to her standards of academic and scientific excellence. Through her enormous fund of knowledge of world art history, her painstaking original research, and her meticulous objectivity, she has done more than any other living scholar to elevate the study of Armenian miniature painting, architecture, and sculpture into a first-class science.

The reader will find here no mere essay of "art appreciation"; rather, a scholarly study of an important example of medieval church decoration. He will find great aesthetic delight in the beautiful photography, but the photographs will assume unusual significance with Miss Der Nersessian's lucid, careful, and detailed analyses and descriptions; her explanations of the important theological implications of the various scenes and figures depicted on the monument; her study of the style of the sculptures and paintings; her investigations of the relations of this edifice to earlier or contemporary monuments, Moslem as well as Christian; and finally her conclusions substantiated by specific comparisons to show the place of the Armenian Church of Aght'amar in the general development of medieval art.

Miss Der Nersessian's book is not only a valuable contribution to the understanding of medieval church decoration and East Christian art; it is, as well, a beautiful resurrection of a long dormant and unseen witness of an ancient culture.

The Harvard Armenian Texts and Studies series will, as the title implies, encompass a broad range of monographic studies in line with the multifaceted direction of the Armenian program. It is hoped that the quality of this first volume, for which the Armenian Studies Funds of Harvard and the Dumbarton Oaks Center for Byzantine Studies in Washington generously provided financial support, will set the standard of the series and become the prelude to continued eminence in future studies.

Avedis K. Sanjian, Chairman
Harvard Armenian Texts and
Studies Committee

Cambridge, Massachusetts
April 1964

PREFACE

In the summer of 1956 four young architects, Peter Ahrend, Richard Burton, John Donat, and Paul Koralek passed by the region of Lake Van on their way to Iran. Their main objective was the study of Seljuk art but they had been interested in the Armenian church of Aght'amar and were anxious to see this monument. Through circumstances beyond their control they could spend barely more than twenty-four hours on the island, but they made excellent use of the short time at their disposal. Their combined efforts and, above all, their systematic and intelligent approach resulted in a complete photographic coverage, with details of almost every section of the sculpture. For the first time also the paintings of the interior, neglected by earlier travelers, were entirely photographed. I wish to express my sincere thanks to them for putting all their material at my disposal, thus enabling me to prepare the present study. Their photographs have been supplemented by some that were taken independently by Miss Josephine Powell; these comprise figures 6, 16, 37, 43–46, 49, 54, 58–59, 61, 67, 69–70, 76.

Production of this book was begun by The Old Bailey Press in London. My manuscript was sent to the press in July 1959 and I corrected the second set of proofs in November 1960; unfortunately, through unforeseen circumstances production was interrupted and was not resumed. Mr. Basil Burton kindly sent me in the summer of 1962 all the negatives, those engraver's blocks that had been made, and the dummy of the plates prepared by Mr. Richard Bouwens. No changes have been made in the text; I have only added in the notes bibliographical references to the studies published since 1959.

My grateful thanks are due to the Department of Near Eastern Languages and Literature of Harvard University for including this book in their series of Armenian Texts and Studies, and to the Dumbarton Oaks Center for Byzantine Studies, Trustees for Harvard University, for the grant of a generous subsidy. In the course of my study I benefited from the discussions with my colleagues at Dumbarton Oaks and Professor André Grabar in Paris. I also wish to thank Miss Marie Edel for reading over my manuscript.

Sirarpie Der Nersessian

Paris, 1964

CONTENTS

ILLUSTRATIONS

40–55. North façade

40. General view of north façade. 41. North façade, central section. 42. Samson killing a Philistine. 43. Samson killing a lion. 44. King Hezekiah. 45. Isaiah. 46. North façade, central section, lower part. 47. Adam and Eve. 48. Eve and the serpent. 49. North façade, right half. 50. St. Theodore killing the dragon, St. Cyriacus. 51. Bear eating grapes, lion attacking a bull. 52. David killing a lion. 53. Vine scroll. 54. Vine scroll. 55. Vine scroll.

56. South door: lintel

57–70. Interior

57. Dome: creation scenes. 58. Dome: creation scenes. 59. South exedra. 60. Northwest view. 61. Northeast view. 62. East apse: Apostles Paul, Andrew, Philip. 63. South exedra, left half: Annunciation, Visitation. 64. West exedra, left half: Joseph's dream, flight into Egypt, Raising of Lazarus, Entry into Jerusalem. 65. West exedra, right half: massacre of innocents, Christ anointed, feet washing. 66. West exedra, pier to the right: mourning mothers. 67. North exedra: Baptism, Transfiguration, wedding at Cana, Crucifixion, holy women at sepulcher, Harrowing of hell. 68. West exedra: Raising of Lazarus, Entry into Jerusalem (color). 69. North exedra: Crucifixion, holy women and apostles at sepulcher. 70. South exedra: Second Coming of Christ.

71–77. Cross stones and tombstones

71. Cross stone of Catholicos Stephen IV, dated 1340, upper half. 72. Cross stone of Catholicos Stephen IV, lower half. 73. Cross stone of Catholicos Zak'aria III, dated 1444. 74. Tombstone. 75. Tombstone of the nineteenth century. 76. Tombstone of the nineteenth century. 77. Tombstones (in color).

AGHT'AMAR
CHURCH OF THE HOLY CROSS

BLACK SEA

Batum

Trebizond

Tiflis

Kura R.

GUGARK'

UTI

L. Sevan

Kars
Ani
Vagharshapat
Erevan
Dvin

ARTSAKH

AYRARAT

SIUNIK'

BARDSR HAYK'

Araxes R.
Mt. Ararat

P'AYTAKARAN

Tchorokh R.
TAYK'

Erzerum

Erzinjan

Araxes R.

TURUBERAN

Mt. Sipan
L. Van

Euphrates R.

Khlat'

Van
Varag

Mush

VASPURAKAN

Bitlis

Aght'amar
Vostan

L. Urmia

AGHDSNIK'

MOKK'

Melitene

Great Zab

Amida

KORDJAIK'
PARSKAHAYK'

Tigris River

Mardin

Nisibis

Edessa

Mossul

Euphrates River

RUSSIA

TURKEY

SYRIA
IRAN
IRAQ

50   0   50   100   200 kilometers

50   0   50   100   150 miles

HISTORICAL BACKGROUND

THE Armenian Church of the Holy Cross is built on the small island of Aght'amar, in Lake Van, in the southeastern part of present-day Turkey, the ancient Armenian province of Vaspurakan. The vast lake, which has an area of about thirteen hundred square miles, is dominated on the north by the lofty slopes of Mount Sipan whose snow-capped peak attains an altitude of thirteen thousand, seven hundred feet; to the southwest rises the mass of Nimrud Dagh, with its gigantic volcanic crater filled by a lake. The city of Van lies in the curve of the southeastern bay of the lake, at the foot of towering rock, the citadel of the ancient Kingdom of Urartu whose kings ruled over the land before the arrival of the Armenians in the latter part of the seventh century B.C. Remains of the massive structures erected by the kings of Urartu are still visible and the rock itself is covered by numerous cuneiform inscriptions incised in the hard stone. In an easterly direction from Van can be seen the limestone ridges of Mount Varag, and on the south the lake is bordered by the dark range of the mountains of Kurdistan.

H. F. B. Lynch, who visited Armenia in 1893–94 and again in 1898, has left a most valuable description of the country and its monuments; he writes of the view from Van. "Of the beauty of the site it would not be possible to speak too highly . . . In the north across the waters is outspread an Italian landscape—a Vesuvius or an Etna, with their sinuous surroundings, on an Asiatic scale. Nearer at hand and fully exposed, the long barrier of the Kurdish mountains recalls the wildest scenery of the Norwegian coast. From the city herself as from the extremities of the wide basin, the short, sharp ridge of Varag is seen with pleasure to the eye, lifted some forty-five hundred feet above the waters, and, at evening, reflecting the sunset in the most varied hues. The lake is not sufficiently large to separate these various objects by distances which preclude under ordinary conditions the simultaneous enjoyment of all from a single shore. And it is large enough to spread at their feet with all the qualities of the ocean— the depth and vastness and changing surfaces of the high seas."[1]

The island of Aght'amar is about two miles from the southern shore of the lake. "At its westerly extremity a bold cliff of hard grey limestone rises to a height of about eighty feet above the waters, in face of the monastic buildings on the mainland. From this crag the ground declines towards the east, and affords a level site for the church and cloister."[2]

Very little is known about the ancient history of the island. The poetic imagination of the people has invented a story to explain the name of Aght'amar (also pronounced Akht'amar), a story which, unconsciously, echoes the Greek legend of Hero and Leander. It is said that a young nobleman was in love with a beautiful girl by the name of T'amar who lived on the island, and every night he came across from the mainland to visit her. One stormy night he struggled in vain against the strong waves and was drowned, gasping "Akh T'amar" with his last breath. The young girl, watching helpless from the opposite shore, died of sorrow at the same time as her lover. From that day on, say the people, the island was called Akht'amar.

In the early Middle Ages the island belonged to the feudal family of the Rshtunik' whose domains extended along the south shores of Lake Van; it was used mostly as a place of refuge at times of invasion and seems to have been strengthened in the seventh century by the Armenian general Theodore Rshtuni. But only in the tenth century did Aght'amar come into prominence. At this time Gagik Artzruni made it into one of the principal seats of his kingdom.

The Artzrunis, who claimed descent from Sennacherib, King of Assyria, did not play a major role in the early history of Armenia; their power grew especially during the latter part of the Arab occupation. They became the suzerains of the Rshtunis and gradually took possession of some of the Rshtuni lands on the south of Lake Van. They extended their domains over the province of Vaspurakan, that is, the entire region east of Lake Van from the Great Zab, a tributary of the Tigris, on the south, almost as far as the river Araxes on the north, and to Lake Urmia on the east. They were the chief rivals of the Bagratids who had first been granted the title of "prince of princes of Armenia, of Georgia, and of the lands of the Caucasus" by the Arab caliph and who, some years later, in 886, were recognized as the kings of Armenia both by the Arabs and the Byzantines. Taking advantage of the enmity between King Smbat and the Arab emir of Azerbaijan, and of the Arab policy which favored now one princely family and now another in order to keep either one of them from becoming too powerful, Gagik obtained from Yusuf the title of King of Vaspurakan, in 908. Yusuf placed on his head "a crown of pure gold and artistic workmanship, adorned with pearls and most precious jewels, which I cannot describe. He clad him in a tunic woven with gold and girt him with a belt and a sword resplendent with gold ornaments beyond imagination and description. Mounted on a horse with gilt trappings, he shone like the sun amid the stars; large companies of soldiers, armed from head to foot, stood to the right and to the left; the weapons clashed, the swords glittered, the trumpets resounded, the horns blared, the flutes shrilled, the lyres gave forth melodious sounds; psalteries and banners preceded and followed him, and the soldiers of the royal army let out a mighty shout which shook the earth. With such pomp was he installed."[3] Shortly after, the caliph himself sent a second crown and costly robes to Gagik.

The contemporary historian Thomas Artzruni and his continuator relate in glowing terms the activities of Gagik, who was an able ruler and during whose reign the province of Vaspurakan became very prosperous despite repeated Arab invasions and internal struggles. They enumerate and at times describe with considerable detail the numerous buildings erected by Gagik, the fortresses which he restored or raised anew, as well as important engineering projects such as the underground stone water conduit which descended from the summit of Mount Varag.[4] Among the churches built while he was still a prince, those erected at the foot of the rock of Amrakan, rising behind Van, deserve particular mention, for they commemorated the holy sites of the Passion and the Resurrection. The main church was dedicated to Holy Zion; at the right of the altar was a chapel named Golgotha and above it another to recall the upper chamber where the apostles had assembled. At the left of the apse was a chapel in memory of Christ's resurrection and above it another dedicated to the Ascension.[5] To all the churches that he built, Gagik donated precious vessels, silver censers, crosses, and gold reliquaries adorned with jewels.

The most important constructions were those of Vostan, on the south shore of Lake Van, and those of the island of Aght'amar. Thomas Artzruni dwells at some length on the beauties of the site of Vostan, surrounded by orchards, vineyards, and springs of fresh water.[6] Behind the city, he writes, rises the high mountain of Artos on which, even in summer, flowers and plants retain their first verdure; from the snow-covered summits flow the murmuring brooks, watering the land and bringing to the lake numerous small fish. Gagik decided to build a palace on a summit from which one could see the lake and watch the rippling waters, and he surrounded the palace and pavilions with beautiful streets. He also raised strong ramparts toward the lake and above these walls a pavilion for gatherings which was adorned with many colors and glittering gold.

But it is the Church of Aght'amar and the various other constructions on the island which are described with the greatest pride and joy. Gagik began by building a wide wall around the island, with high towers which provided pleasant retreats where the king liked to rest, in the company of his sons and courtiers.[7] At one end of the island two walls projected into the sea and almost joined, enclosing the waters and thus providing a safe harbor for ships. Gagik wished to make of Aght'amar a refuge for everyone. The work was carried on with such speed that within five years a new city had come into existence. The king himself, writes Thomas, assisted by many craftsmen, planned and designed, at the foot of the mountain which formed the culminating point of the island, places for enjoyment; he laid out the streets, the terraced gardens, the orchards; he planted numerous trees which were watered by the never failing spring which divine providence had caused to gush forth in the midst of the city. Many craftsmen were assembled at the royal gate, honorable men who had come from all parts and were ready to carry out the king's plans. Gagik commanded one of them, a wise and gifted architect, to erect a palace for him. This was a square structure, forty cubits in length and width as well as in height, and its thick walls made of solid blocks of stone and lime were like molten lead and copper that have been fused together. The main hall, surrounded by numerous vaulted exedrae and square rooms, all of them richly decorated, rose "from the foundations to the summit, like the sheer flight of a bird" without any columnar supports. The high dome, resembling the dome of heaven, was decorated with gold and shone with brilliant light; "if one wishes to look at it," writes Thomas, "he must first remove his cap, as if he were honoring a king, then, twisting his neck, he will barely be able to distinguish the many beautiful representations. This palace is so impressive and amazing in its structure, and surpasses so greatly one's imagination, that even an intelligent man after spending many hours looking at only one of the pavilions, would not be able to relate, when he went out, all that he had seen. For one sees represented here gilt thrones on which the king is seated in elegant majesty, surrounded by brilliant-faced young men, attendants of his rejoicings, also by groups of musicians and young girls dancing in an admirable manner. There are represented also companies of men with bared swords and combats of wrestlers; groups of lions and other wild beasts; flocks of birds of rich and varied plumage. Should one wish to enumerate all that is depicted here, this would entail great labor on his part and on that of his listeners."[8]

The palace was visible from all sides and appeared like a hill in the middle of the city, no less high than the rocky promontory on the other end of the island. Gagik also built on the island various magazines, storehouses, buildings for his treasures and for all types of arms and armors.

At the time when all this work was being carried on at Aght'amar, Gagik had led an expedition against some unruly tribes who were settled close to the Assyrian border, in a village called Kotom; he razed their fortress and carried the stones, by sea, to the island of Aght'amar so that they might be used for the construction of the church he wished to found. "The architect, who was Manuel, as mentioned above,[9] was a learned man, most proficient in his art, and he built a remarkable church with consummate skill. He entrusted the cleric, whom we mentioned above, with the sculptural decoration which depicted, in true likeness, all the figures beginning with Abraham and David until Our Lord Jesus Christ and the groups of prophets and apostles, each one of them admirable in appearance. He also devised and depicted around the church companies of game animals and flocks of birds, also all varieties of wild beasts, boars and lions, bulls and bears facing one another, recalling the opposition of their natures which greatly pleases wise men. He girded the church with a remarkable and detailed frieze, which represented a grape vine animated with figures of vintagers, with wild animals and reptiles, accurately rendering the characteristics of each species.

"And on the four façades, at the summit of the exedrae, he depicted the lifelike portraits of the four evangelists, who are, in truth, the crowns of joy of the holy church and higher than all the saints.

"He represented on the wall of the west exedra the cross-nimbed image of the Saviour, who was incarnate for our sake and assumed human form. Facing the Saviour is the true likeness and glorious image of King Gagik who, with proud faith, raises in his hands [the model of] the church, like a gold vase full of manna, or like a gold casket filled with perfume; he stands before the Lord in the attitude of a man begging for the remission of his sins. These are our words, but the king will surely not be denied the gifts he requests, having faith in the rewards of the hereafter.

"To the south side of the apse, above the entrance of the church, is the royal gallery, reached by means of a vaulted staircase; this is the place where the king prays, removed and isolated from others, so that he may converse with God undisturbed.

"And in the interior, he fashioned the marvelous holy of holies, adorned with paintings and with silver doors, and filled with chased gold ornaments, images covered with gold, precious stones and pearls, and all kinds of marvelous and brilliant vessels which recall, in glorious fashion, the second Jerusalem and also the gate of Zion on high.

"Thus are fulfilled the prophetic songs: 'rejoice mountain and thirsty desert,' or again 'the earth shall rejoice and the many islands shall be filled with gladness.' For, verily, this was once a thirsty desert, and it is now the city of God, watered by two fountains, ever gushing forth from the holy font and the incorruptible blood of the Son of God, to quench the thirst of the soul.

"And on the day of the dedication, a great and joyful feast was celebrated, graced by numerous bishops and princes, the memory of which will be perpetuated from generation to generation."

The dates generally accepted for the construction of the Church of the Holy Cross at Aght'amar are 915 to 921, although this is not mentioned by Thomas Artzruni. The information is derived from a text compiled at the end of the eighteenth century and completed in the early nineteenth century, giving a list of the catholicoses of Aght'amar. Although this text, the work of an ignorant man, is full of errors, the dates of the construction of the church may be correct, being based perhaps on the long inscription on the west façade, now hidden by the forechurch.[10]

The small kingdom of Vaspurakan which Gagik had enlarged, strengthened, and endowed with fine monuments lasted for less than a century after his death in 936. Weakened by foreign wars and internal strife it was unable to offer adequate resistance to the new wave of invaders who harassed the country slaughtering the inhabitants and destroying everything in their way. Faced with disaster, King Senek'erim lent a favorable ear to the proposals of the Byzantines who aimed to take possession of all the Armenian principalities and had already begun their program of annexation. In 1021 he ceded his kingdom to Basil II, receiving in exchange the city of Sebastia, in Cappadocia, and the surrounding territory as far as the Euphrates. A veritable exodus took place at this time; the continuator of Thomas Artzruni writes that 14,000 persons, not counting women and children, followed the king. But Byzantium was not able to retain for a long period its new possessions; the crushing defeat at the battle of Mantzikert, north of Lake Van, in 1071 sealed the doom of Byzantine rule in Armenia and the entire country fell into the power of the Turcomans.

In the province of Vaspurakan two strongholds still remained in Armenian hands: the fortress of Amiuk, above Van, and the island of Aght'amar, both of them held by a descendant of the Artzrunis. Many of the precious relics of the Armenian church, some of which had been taken from Ani, the capital and the see of the catholicos, the supreme head of the church, were deposited at Aght'amar, and in 1113 the bishopric of Aght'amar was raised to the rank of a catholicosate, thus creating a rival see which caused serious dissension within the Armenian church.[11]

Very little is known about the early history of this new see and only toward the latter part of the thirteenth century do we begin to have definite information, primarily through the colophons or notices added by the scribes to the manuscripts which they copied. The scriptorium of Aght'amar was very productive, especially in the fifteenth and sixteenth centuries;

a number of the manuscripts written at that time have survived and many of them are illustrated. In the course of time new structures were erected. In 1293 a chapel, dedicated to St. Stephen, was built to the southeast of the main church;[12] a few years later the Catholicos Zacharias I built a large oratory for the winter season, close to the Church of the Holy Cross and, on the west side, another oratory for the summer season, a vaulted structure the stones of which had been brought from Khlat', on the north shore of Lake Van.[13] In the late eighteenth century additions were made to the Church of the Holy Cross, which will be mentioned below.

King Gagik had been well inspired when he raised his most important building on the island of Aght'amar for though fairly close to the shore, it was still beyond the route of the invaders and was thus saved from the sad fate which befell most of the churches built on the mainland. We do not know when the palace of Gagik and the other secular buildings were destroyed; however the church in which he took such pride stands to this day, perpetuating the memory of his name, but abandoned and silent, ever since the entire Armenian population was driven from this region. The walls no longer echo the chants of the religious services which were celebrated there for almost a thousand years, yet in some intangible way the island still retains a feeling of its past glories and impressed those who visited it in recent years.

The island of Aght'amar lying off the main routes to the Orient was not visited by European travelers before the middle of the nineteenth century. In 1850 the Assyriologist Austen Layard passed by the region of Van on his way back from Mesopotamia and it was through his brief description of the Church of Aght'amar that Western scholars first became aware of its existence.[14] Half a century passed before another Englishman, H. F. B. Lynch, visited the island and gave a more detailed description accompanied by several views of the church.[15] The archaeological studies of the monument began with Walter Bachmann, who published the plan of the main church and subsidiary chapels as well as better reproductions of the sculptures and a view of the interior.[16] In his important work on Armenian architecture Joseph Strzygowski devoted a great deal of attention to the sculptures and to the architecture[17] of the church, and since then this monument has been mentioned in all the general books dealing with East Christian art. During these same years when European scholars had become interested in Aght'amar, the church had also been described in a number of Armenian books,[18] of which the most important is the detailed description published by E. Lalayan, and accompanied by a rough plan and several views.[19] In recent years the rich sculptural decoration has been discussed in several articles, in particular those of A. Sakisian, of Coche de la Ferté, of R. Burton, J. Donat, and P. Koralik, and of myself.[20] The sculptures have also been discussed by Goyan in a work devoted to the history of the Armenian theater.[21] Thus the Church of Aght'amar is not an obscure monument, but the present work is the first detailed study of it as a whole, including also the paintings which had barely been mentioned heretofore.

THE ARCHITECTURE

THE Church of the Holy Cross,* built of carefully joined pink sandstone facing an inner core of rubble concrete, is a small building, 14.80 meters long and 11.50 meters wide in the interior. The plan is of the centralized type which, with certain variations, had been in use in Armenia since the seventh century, and even earlier. The large central square, crowned with a dome, is buttressed by four semicircular axial exedrae, and by four small diagonal niches in the form of three-quarter cylinders. The niches at the east end give access to two subsidiary chambers which flank the east exedra, the apse, but do not open into it. When the church was still in use, a relic of the True Cross was kept in the right lateral chamber, and liturgical vessels were housed in the left one. The east and west exedrae are deeper than the other two because of the intervention of arches between them and the central space. At the east the exedra and its arch combine to form the sanctuary; the floor level is raised here and made accessible by four steps from either side. At the west a narrow continuous recess between the exedra and its arch serves to separate these two elements. The south exedra housed the king's gallery, supported by the roof of the apse, the conch, over the entrance. The gallery's stone balustrade, preserved until recent years, was richly decorated with pomegranate branches, carved in relief around a five-arched opening, and with six animal heads in the round; these represented an ox, a ram, a tiger, a stag, an elephant, and a calf.[22] The outer staircase which originally led to the gallery was destroyed in the nineteenth century when a belfry was added in front of the south entrance.

The dome, the crown of which rises 20.40 meters above the ground, rests on a high circular drum, and this, in turn, rests on four pendentives. These pendentives, or inverted spherical triangles, do not taper to a point, as is customary, for the arched openings of the diagonal niches cut into their bases. Consequently the weight of the dome is distributed among the eight pier supports between the axial exedrae and the diagonal niches (fig. 59).

The church is well lighted by means of eight windows pierced in the drum and sixteen others which open into the exedrae and niches. The principal entrance is through the west exedra; there are also two others through the south and north exedrae.

As is so often the case in Armenian architecture, the exterior only partially reflects the inner forms of the church. The east end has a rectangular shape, for the apse and the subsidiary chambers are buried in the thickness of the walls and only deep wedge-shaped recesses suggest a separation between the central and lateral units. By breaking the monotony of a uniform surface, these recesses contribute to the general decorative effect. The west end, narrower than the east end, also has a rectangular shape; here, the recesses mark the width of the exedra. The contours of the north and south façades are much more varied and express better the inner structure of the church. Polygonal walls surround the central exedrae and the southwest

* See plan, p. 9.

and northwest niches; at the east end, where the outer walls of the lateral chambers abut against the niches, the contours of the niches are much simpler. The projecting and retreating walls of these façades, with planes set at different angles, add greatly to the beauty of the exterior, through the changing play of light and shade (figs. 2, 15, 31, 40).

The dome is covered by a conical roof, a typical shape in Armenian churches, and the drum is a sixteen-sided polygon; conical or semiconical roofs also crown the diagonal niches. The gabled roof of the exedrae express, on the exterior, the basic cruciform plan of the church. On the east end the roof covers both the apse and the lateral chambers; consequently it comes down lower than on the other façades, the eaves being immediately above the level of the vine scroll (fig. 31).

An inscription imbedded under the vine scroll of the south façade, above the figures of Saul and David (fig. 23), records that the dome had fallen and was rebuilt. The destruction must have affected only the crown of the dome, for the drum retains its original carved decoration, including the animal frieze immediately under the conical roof (fig. 30). This inscription covers three small rectangular stones and must have extended across a fourth one on the right for the lines are incomplete at this end. There are obvious signs of disturbance in this area up to the edge of the south wall; the stones are smaller and show traces of tooling which do not occur on the surface of the other stones of the façade. It is probable, therefore, that in the course of some later repairs the fourth inscribed stone was replaced by a plain one. The stones have also suffered from weathering, and the text is not very legible. The parts which can be deciphered are as follows:

IN THE VICTORIOUS REIGN OF . . .
KHAN AND IN THE YEAR OF THE ARMENIAN ERA SEVEN HUNDRED . . .
ANOS CATHOLICOS OF THE ARMENIANS IN THE EIGHTH YEAR . . .
. . . I RESTORED THE DOME . . .
. . . BUILT FROM THE FOUNDATIONS . . .
GAGIK KING OF THE ARMENIANS, WHOEVER . . . .
REMEMBERED IN THE LORD.

Part of the date of the reconstruction, the name of the ruling khan, and the beginning of the name of the catholicos must have been on the lost stone. The list of the catholicoses of the see of Aght'amar enables us to complete the name, for only that of Step'anos fits with the last four letters 'anos' which are preserved. The date, given as usual by letters, is that of the Armenian era, and the only remaining letter corresponds to 700; to this 551 must be added to obtain the corresponding year of the Christian era, and this gives us the year 1251, but the letter indicating the hundreds must have been followed by one or two others, corresponding to the decimals and units, so that we must think of a year between 700 and 799, that is between 1251 and 1350. Two catholicoses named Step'anos lived during this period: Step'anos III, 1272–ca.1296 and Step'anos IV, ca.1336–1346. The rule of the former, who had erected the

Church of St. Stephen in 1293, coincides with the reigns of the great Ilkhans of Persia, Abaga, Arghun, and Ghazan (1265–1304), any one of whom could be called a victorious khan, while this term would hardly be used for the puppet rulers who occupied the throne during the troubled years following the death of Abu Said in 1335. Thus it seems probable that the catholicos mentioned in the inscription was Step'anos III. This is corroborated by the notice in a manuscript copied at Aght'amar in 1471, a Ritual for the consecration of the catholicos and the coronation services. In the memorial, or colophon, the scribe gives a brief history of the catholicoses of Aght'amar and states that Step'anos (III) rebuilt the dome of the church and its roof.[23]

Except for this reconstruction and minor repairs carried out in the course of centuries, the plan and the structure have remained unchanged. But subsidiary buildings, erected at different periods, unfortunately modify the general effect and diminish the impression of great elegance and harmony which the church must have made when it rose unencumbered by these later additions. The small vaulted basilica on the northeast angle may be one of the oratories which, as mentioned above, was built by the Catholicos Zacharias (1296–1336).

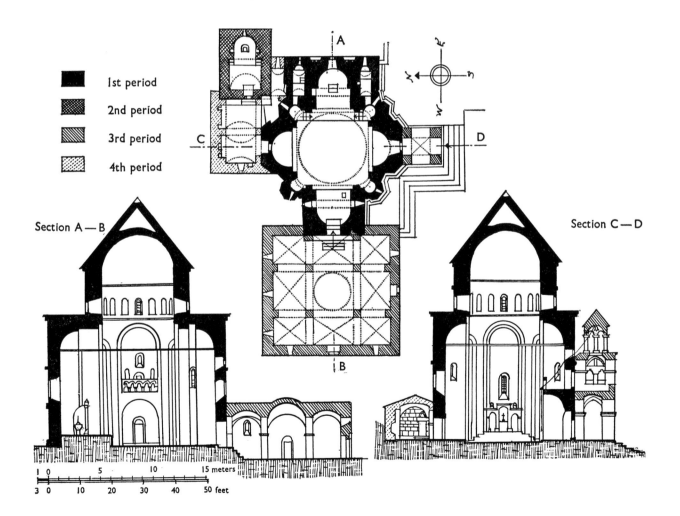

1st period
2nd period
3rd period
4th period

Section A — B

Section C — D

0 5 10 15 meters
0 10 20 30 40 50 feet

The forechurch, connecting the chapel with the north exedra of the church, was added at a later date. Its roof is level with the palmette scroll which girds the church; the chapel itself is somewhat higher (fig. 2).

A large forechurch was added in front of the west entrance in 1763 by the Catholicos Thomas.[24] Its width is equal to the north-south axis of the church, and its east end abuts against the side walls of the west exedra. The floor level is lower, and four steps lead from the forechurch into the church itself. The building, covered with a low central dome and eight groin vaults, is approximately three meters high; the flat roof comes to the level of the palmette scroll. In the late eighteenth or early nineteenth century, the staircase leading to the king's gallery was destroyed and a belfry, crowned with a lantern, was built in front of the south entrance. The piers and the first story of this belfry abut against the walls of the church and cover some of the carvings; but the lintel over the south entrance is still partly visible (figs. 15, 56).

The niche-buttressed, radiating plan adopted at Aght'amar is one of the favorite forms of Armenian church architecture. Variations of this scheme are to be found in a number of outstanding monuments of the seventh century. As at the church of St. Hrip'sime, erected in 618 at Vagharshapat, three-quarter cylinder niches alternate with the axial exedrae, but at Aght'amar the angle chambers of the west end have been eliminated, as they had also been at Artik, and the niches which flank the apse are smaller and rectangular in plan.[25] It is primarily in the treatment of the enveloping walls, especially those of the north and south façades, that Aght'amar differs from these earlier examples. The small niches project on the exterior, the varied contour line with the retreating planes which create contrasting areas of light and shade, adds to the aesthetic effect, and provides a more extensive surface for the carved decoration.

THE SCULPTURE

DESCRIPTION   FIGURE sculpture appeared at an early date on the façades of Armenian churches, but it was usually restricted to the tympanum, the lintel, and the archivolts around the windows, as at Ptghni, K'asakh, and Mren, or introduced between the arches of a decorative arcade, as at Zvart'nots.[26] Aght'amar is a unique example at this date, not only in Armenia but also in the entire Christian world, of a church covered with carvings. Not until the Romanesque period, more than a century later, do we find other monuments with such a rich display of figure and ornamental sculpture.

The decoration is partly subordinated to the architectural forms, outlining the principal elements, but for the most part the walls are treated as a uniform surface which can be covered, at will, with various representations. An animal frieze is carved in high relief, immediately under the conical roof of the dome (figs. 2, 15, 30, 40); lions, foxes, dogs, hares, gazelles, and a horse pursue one another in rapid motion, interrupted here and there by confronted groups, by birds, and by human masks. A scalloped band, with small three-lobed leaves lodged between the scallops, girds the base of the drum of the dome, and a second animal frieze is carved under the eaves of the roofs of the exedrae and niches. Here, in addition to the animals mentioned above, one can also see oxen, panthers, ibexes, and serpents, occasionally interrupted by confronted or fighting animals, by human masks, and by stylized floral designs. Human masks are aligned under the eaves of the west exedra (figs. 16, 30, 40). On the north wall of the exedra there are five female masks, with long hair, and five male ones, four of them bearded and the central one beardless. On the south wall of the exedra two beardless heads cut immediately below the neck and seen in profile are inserted among the male masks. Crouching lions form the consoles at the west end of these two walls, and next to them, on the west wall, are two feminine masks, larger than the others; the one on the left is nimbed (fig. 30). There is no animal frieze on the north and south walls of the east exedra, for there the roof comes down to the level of the vine scroll.

This vine scroll, animated with various scenes and figures which will be described in detail, encircles the façades at a distance of about one meter from the animal frieze; on the west and east façades it is raised higher in the center. Another ornamental band girds the lower parts of the walls, at a height of approximately three meters from the ground. It consists of interlacing circles, with split palmettes framing large clusters of grapes inside each circle. Pine cones are lodged between the circles both above and below, and a simple palmette scroll is carved on the upper and lower faces of this projecting band. Animals, some of which are carved in the round, and a rich array of human figures, to be described in detail, fill the spaces between the vine and palmette scrolls. Arched bands, decorated with different combinations of vegetable scrolls, crown the windows of the drum and those of the church, as well as the triangular recesses on the west and east façades.

West façade (figs. 3–14). The standing figure of the evangelist Matthew, holding the book of the Gospels and blessing, is carved under the gable of the roof (fig. 3); below, the portraits of King Gagik and Jesus flank the central window (figs. 5, 7–9). Gagik holds with his left hand the model of the church which he presents to Jesus; in spite of its damaged condition one can see that this model was a faithful copy of the actual monument, showing the west façade with its two windows, one above the other, and the two triangular recesses (figs. 5, 7). Gagik is clad in a heavy mantle and a long tunic below which one can barely see the edge of his trousers; he wears soft leather shoes. The tunic, slit below the knees in front and with flaps turned back showing the plain lining, is decorated with rows of concentric and interlocking circles between narrow vertical bands. The mantle is attached on the breast with a brooch in the shape of a rosette. The design of the rich material, edged with a triple band, consists of interlocking circles formed by two continuous strands; each circle frames a bird, turned sometimes to the right, sometimes to the left, and five-lobed leaves fill the lozenge-shaped spaces between the circles. Gagik's crown is partly broken, but there still remain the wide circular band, surmounted by a half-rosette and two semicircular motifs, and the winglike motif on the right side (fig. 9). The holes drilled on the circular band and the semicircular motif on the left are probably meant to suggest precious stones; there is also a row of holes, between double bands, around his nimbus. Jesus, slightly shorter than Gagik (figs. 5, 8), stands full face, blessing and holding a closed book on which are inscribed the words "I am the light of the world" (John 8.12). His nimbus is edged with small holes; the inscribed cross stands out in higher relief; and His name is carved above His head. Two angels, holding a medallion with a cross, fill the space between Jesus and Gagik (figs. 5, 10). The cross, covered with a twisted-rope motif or guilloche, has flaring arms terminating in small knobs; it is framed by half-palmettes, and lotus buds fill the spaces between the arms. Two seraphim, their six wings covered with eyes, are carved beyond the triangular recesses; the hands of the one on the left are hidden under his wings, while the one on the right raises his arms in the gesture of adoration (figs. 5, 6). The three large crosses carved below the level of the upper window (figs. 5, 11, 12) differ in shape from the one held by the angels; the ends of the arms do not flare quite as much, the lower arm is slightly longer than the others and it, alone, is framed by half-palmettes which bear bunches of grapes; there are no lotus buds. The lateral crosses are set in frames, and five-lobed leaves, placed diagonally, fill the upper angles (fig. 12). Two small birds are perched on the lateral arms of the central cross. At a short distance, on either side, are two lion heads, carved in the round; these are now badly damaged (fig. 5).

In the central part of the vine scroll, carved above the window, the branches, laden with heavy bunches of grapes, wind around a pomegranate tree; two small birds stand symmetrically on either side (fig. 3). The horizontal bands are animated with human figures and beasts (figs. 13, 14). Proceeding from left to right we see: a human head above the vine branch; a large seated deer and a fawn; a bear eating grapes with a small suckling cub between her legs and another cub perched on her back; a man, turned to the right, holding a large pumpkin.

The horizontal band on the right is half a stone course higher (figs. 4, 14). A man, clad only in short trousers, struggles with a bear; a man, wearing a long tunic and seated on the ground, holds the vine branches around one of which he has passed his left leg; two small goats butt their heads against each other; an archer, wearing a close-fitting tunic kneels on one knee and shoots an arrow at a bear; the bear rears on its hind legs, and its shoulder has already been pierced by an arrow.

Stylized pomegranate trees cover the arches which crown the wedge-shaped recesses (figs. 5, 13, 14). The root of one tree fills the short horizontal band on each side, and the stem, with alternating fruits and leaves, curves upward; two confronted birds are carved at the meeting point of the trees on the left arch, and a seven-lobed leaf on the right arch. Palmette scrolls are carved on the intrados and extrados of these arches, and a slightly more ornate palmette scroll covers the arch which crowns the central window (figs. 5, 11). Palmette leaves, in a heart-shaped frame, also crown the inner curve of each wedge-shaped recess (figs. 13, 14).

South façade (figs. 15–29). The figure of the evangelist carved below the gable is only partly visible behind the lantern of the modern belfry; he probably represents St. Luke (fig. 16). The Biblical scenes and single figures follow one another without marked separation between them. Beginning again at the left we see, first of all, several episodes of the story of Jonah which fill the entire side wall of the exedra (fig. 17). Three nude men stand inside a U-shaped boat which has a large sail hanging like a curtain from a slightly curved horizontal spar attached to the mast. One of the men has seized Jonah, who is also nude, and is casting him into the gaping jaws of the whale which lies on its back, immediately under the boat; the sea has not been represented (fig. 18). In the lower zone of the next section the whale is depicted like the mythical winged sea lion; a small fish is carved under it. Though the monster has its jaws wide open, the figure of Jonah being ejected has not been represented; we see the prophet farther to the right, reclining on top of the gourd tree instead of under it (fig. 19). In the upper zone Jonah, clothed, addresses the King of Nineveh, who is seated on two cushions placed on the ground. To the right four medallions frame the busts of three bearded men and one beardless youth. The youth points to Jonah and the King; the other three, with sorrowful expressions, raise their right hands to their faces. The four other medallions with bust portraits, grouped above (fig. 17), do not form part of the Jonah cycle; the inscriptions identify the first two as Stephen the protomartyr and Zephaniah, and the last as Elijah. The third saint is youthful and he wears a chlamys like the military saints.

The sacrifice of Isaac is carved on the left side of the polygonal wall of the southwest niche (figs. 17, 22). Isaac, clad in a long tunic, kneels on a rectangular stone altar, his hands are tied behind his back. Abraham has grasped Isaac by the hair; knife in hand, he is about to slay him. Abraham turns his head sharply toward the hand of God, emerging from above, and toward the ram hanging by its horns from the tree. Abraham's and Isaac's names are inscribed above them.

On the adjoining wall of the niche, to the left of the window crowned with an ornate band, stands a large nimbed figure who, with veiled hands, raises a rectangular object. Although there is no accompanying inscription, the figure can only be Moses with the Tables of the Law (fig. 17). Two confronted goats, forelegs pressed against a palm tree and heads turned backwards, fill the space under the window (fig. 17). To the right of this window is a large angel turned toward the enthroned Christ carved on the short wall between the niche and the exedra (figs. 17, 20). Christ, blessing, holds against His knee a book stamped with a large cross. The throne, covered with geometric designs, has an ornate cushion but no back; the columns of the canopy are also decorated with geometric figures while the arch is covered with a palmette scroll. The large initials of Christ are carved above His head.

The group of the Virgin and Child between archangels, carved on the side walls of the exedra, face, at an angle, the figures of Christ and the angel (figs. 17, 21). The inscriptions on the scrolls identify the archangels as Gabriel, on the left, and Michael, on the right. The Virgin's throne has a high back, slightly curved on the top; the uprights terminating in round knobs are also decorated with geometric motifs; the footstool is edged with small holes. The Christ Child, seated on His mother's left knee, holds a closed scroll. The inscription above the throne reads "Mary, Mother of God." Christ's initials are also carved.

Only two of the four saints represented above these groups are identified: the prophet Joel, in the second medallion, and the prophet Nahum, in the fourth one (fig. 17). The youthful figure next to Nahum seems to be addressing him; only the lower half of his medallion has been carved.

The last carvings visible to the left of the belfry represent an ibex and, below, two confronted eagles standing on the volutes of a stylized plant and biting a ring (fig. 17).[27] On the lintel of the south door, still partly visible, is carved a large rosette between two crosses similar to the ones on the west façade (fig. 56). According to Lalayan, one can also see, at the sides of the door opening into the king's gallery, a lion and a tiger, heads bent in sign of obedience, and, above these animals, two saints, a deer, and an eagle.[28]

The carvings on the east half of the south façade, beyond the belfry, can be divided into two groups: those which cover the polygonal walls of the exedra and the southeast niche, and those which fill the side wall of the east end (fig. 23). In the first section real and imaginary animals frame the standing figures of two saints. On the left are represented a griffon and two confronted bears with two confronted hares lodged between their legs; on the right are a large bird with a horned head and an eagle striking a small bird (figs. 28, 29). The two saints, who face each other at an angle, are identified by the inscription as "Lord Saint Sahak, brother of Hamazasp, martyrs and witnesses of Christ" and "Lord Saint Hamazasp, prince of Vaspurakan." These two princes of the Artzruni family were put to death in 786 by the Arabs because they would not abjure the Christian faith, and their memory is recorded in the Armenian martyrology. Sahak wears a long coat, like a kaftan, which crosses diagonally on the breast and is fastened at the waist by a heavy metal belt with three pendants (fig. 24). The skirt of the coat is turned back, showing the plain lining, and his plain undergarment can be seen at the V-shaped opening of the neck. The coat is decorated with rows of small concentric circles separated from one another by means of vertical and horizontal double lines. Hamazasp holds a small cross (fig. 25). His coat, decorated with a diaper design of crosses, has no belt; it is slit in front, below the knees, and the flaps are turned back showing the plain lining. The edge of his trousers is visible under the coat. Rectangular pieces of plain material are sewn on the front of the coat, above the waist; the edges are turned back to form the lapels and a narrow collar. Both brothers wear soft leather shoes.

None of the saints represented in the three medallions above these groups is identified. Above one window, which is crowned with a palmette scroll, the bust figure of the high priest Eli is carved on a rectangular slab, without any frame. He is turned to the right and seems to be gazing at the scene of David's fight against Goliath, represented on the east end of this façade (fig. 23).

The giant figure of Goliath, almost two meters high, stands on the extreme right; his name is inserted next to him: "Goliath, the foreigner" (fig. 27). In conformity with the Biblical text, he has "an helmet of brass upon his head" and is "armed with a coat of mail" (I Samuel 17.5). His coat is of plate armor and his shoulders are covered with chain armor; his tunic comes below the knees and he wears high boots of soft leather. Goliath has raised his large sword; with his left hand he holds an embossed shield and what is probably meant to represent his spear, for he had come "with a sword, and with a spear, and with a shield" (17.45). David, bare-legged and wearing a short tunic, faces Goliath; the shepherd's bag in which he had put the "smooth stones out of the brook" hangs from his shoulder and he holds the sling with one stone in it. The backward movement of his arm and the direction of his glance clearly indicate that he is about to throw it. The inscription next to his head reads "the prophet David." The bust figure in the medallion is identified as "the prophet Samuel," and behind David stands "Saul, King of Israel" (figs. 23, 26). Saul has the appearance of an Oriental ruler: he has a turban on his head; his coat, held at the waist by a metal belt with three pendants, is identical in shape with the one worn by Prince Sahak, but the design of the material consists of horizontal bands of palmette scrolls, leaf ornaments, and simple geometric motifs. The sleeping deer, represented between David and Goliath, and the rosettes carved above it have no apparent connection with the scene.[29]

The vine scroll on this façade is peopled with a rich variety of scenes and single figures moving in opposite directions (figs. 15–17). A young shepherd carries a ram on his shoulders. A man is attacked by a bear; he has fallen on his back and while he pushes the beast with his right leg he also tries to stab it with two large knives. Two human heads appear in the loops formed by the vine stock; a bearded man, half seated, half kneeling, raises his hands in a gesture of surprise; two birds flank a palm tree; a man stands probably facing an animal which is not visible on the photograph (figs. 16, 17). Next comes a bear eating grapes. A bearded man, seated on the ground, holds the branches of the vine which frame his head; beside him is a bird. A young man, carrying a sling and a stick, faces a lion. Two cocks stand confronted; a hind turns her head toward her suckling fawn; a young man, one knee on the ground, struggles with a bull which he has seized by the horns. Two men are wrestling; the one on the left has grabbed his opponent's beard and left foot, and a dog runs between their legs. A bird and a human head appear in the loops formed by the vine branches.

The belfry hides from view the central section of the vine scroll. One can see on the extreme right two men standing under arches and beyond it, along the east half of the façade, the following compositions (fig. 23). A man, kneeling, balances a basket on his left shoulder; a human head appears above the vine branches; a boy rides on the back of a bear which he has seized by the ears; a man, one knee on the ground, pierces a bear with his spear; again a bearded head appears above the vine branches; a sphinx stands next to a palm tree from which the fruit hangs in clusters; a bird pecks at the grapes; a man, carrying a stick from which hangs a hare, looks at another hare eating grapes; a young boy appears to be throwing a stone at a bird pecking at the grapes; a fox is eating grapes, and a young man and a running dog approach him from the right.

Some of the animals and animal heads, carved in relief or in the round, are badly damaged and a few are almost completely destroyed. Proceeding once again from left to right we see (figs. 15–17): a bird, whose head is broken off; a stag, running; a human-headed bird; an eagle seen full-face; a lion (?), whose head is broken off; a peacock. In the eastern half of this façade there are only a human head, a guinea hen, and a lion head (fig. 23).

East façade (figs. 31–39). As on the other façades, an evangelist, blessing and holding a book stamped with a cross, is represented under the gable (fig. 31). The inscription is not visible, but as it is the portrait of a beardless man, he can be identified as St. John. The medallion above the central window frames the bust of Adam, represented as an old man with long hair falling on his shoulders (figs. 31, 34, 39). His name is inscribed inside the medallion and next to the medallion are the words "and Adam gave names to all the animals and wild beasts" (Genesis 2.20). Single figures and medallion portraits are symmetrically disposed on the lower parts of this façade (fig. 31). On the left we see first John the Baptist, whose name is carved on a projecting stone (fig. 32). Above him and slightly to the right stands "Saint Gregory, illuminator of the Armenians," clothed in bishop's robes and holding a book stamped with a cross. The youthful saint represented in the medallion is not identified. A lion stands below St. Gregory's feet. The cross carved in low relief is a later addition; the accompanying inscription states that it was carved for one Kirakos in 1721.

On the extreme right of the façade the prophet Elijah stands in an attitude almost identical with that of John the Baptist; his name is also inscribed on a projecting stone (fig. 33); the woman kneeling at his feet must be the widow of Sarepta whose son he healed (I Kings 17). The saint whose position corresponds to that of Gregory the Illuminator is not identified, but is probably St. Thomas; he is clothed in the classical garb of the apostles and he holds a small open scroll in his left hand; he is considerably smaller than the other figures. The two bust figures are also unidentified; the bearded saint is carved on a rectangular slab, the youthful one is framed by a medallion.

The central window is flanked by two standing figures: on the left a man wearing the classical costume of the apostles; on the right a bishop holding a book stamped with a cross with flaring arms (figs. 31, 34, 35). Further down are three animals: a lion which faces the lion carved to the left of the triangular recess, and a leopard and a deer turned to the right (figs. 34, 36).

The central section of the vine scroll rests immediately on the arches which crown the wedge-shaped recesses (figs. 37, 39). A crowned man, holding a wine glass and plucking grapes, is seated cross-legged on a cushion and waited on by two attendants. The one on the right is presenting a fruit (or a cup?); he wears long trousers and a heavy coat clasped at the waist by a belt with three jeweled pendants. The flaps of the coat are turned back to form the lapels and a narrow collar, and one flap of the coat is also turned back below the belt. The man on the left stands next to a pomegranate tree and plucks a fruit; over his trousers he wears a long tunic, clasped at the waist by a jeweled belt with three pendants. Behind him is a fierce-looking lion.

The two side sections of the scroll differ from one another. On the right we have the usual vine scroll: a man is seated in the first circumvolution; in the next one a man digs with a spade (fig. 31). On the left side of the façade the circumvolution closest to the arch is almost intact, and shows a man armed with a stick pursuing a hare (fig. 38). There is also a small section of the scroll on the extreme left, but in the intervening space the vine is replaced by a mounted archer whose head projects into the upper stone course. This rider, who has markedly Mongolian features, wears a large helmet which comes down on his ears and a short tunic which crosses diagonally from left to right. He is armed with a bow, and turns around to shoot an arrow at a bear standing on its hind legs. A narrow vertical stone, wedged between this section and the scroll, cuts off the rear part of the bear.

There are obvious signs of damage and disturbance in this area and, so far as can be determined without a direct examination of the monument, it would seem that the archer and bear have replaced a broken section of the vine scroll. This conclusion is based on the following facts: this is the only place where an element of the frieze projects above the single stone course; the small section of the vine on the extreme left would have no meaning if it were not part of the continuous scroll; the style of the horse and especially of the archer differs from that of the other sculptures of Aght'amar. The Mongolian facial type of the rider, his costume, and his attitude relate this figure to several sculptures executed in the northern provinces of Armenia in the early fourteenth century, during the period of Mongol suzerainty.[30] The imitation of Mongolian types also appears in manuscripts illustrated in the general area of Lake Van during the fourteenth century, and it seems quite probable that the group of the archer and bear was substituted about this time for the damaged part of the scroll.

The foreparts of various animals, some of them too badly damaged to allow identification, are carved in the round on either side of the façade, below the vine scroll; two lion heads flank the medallion of Adam (figs. 31, 37). As on the west façade, pomegranate trees cover the arches which crown the triangular recesses, and a rich vine scroll covers the arch over the central window (figs. 31, 34, 37). Palmette scrolls are again carved on the extrados and intrados of all these arches.

North façade (figs. 40–55). The roof of the forechurch of the small chapel comes up to the level of the palm frieze, and the grass and shrubs now growing on this roof occasionally cover the lowest zone of the sculpture.

The standing figure of St. Mark, identified by the inscription, is carved under the gable; his face and part of his right arm are broken off (fig. 41). The scenes and figures on this façade are as follows, always proceeding from left to right. Samson kills a Philistine (Judges 15.15). Samson is almost as tall as the corresponding image of Goliath on the south façade; he is bare-legged and over his short tunic he wears a mantle which is attached by a wide diagonal strap and hangs behind his back (fig. 42). He has seized the Philistine by the hair and raises the ass's jaw bone in his right hand; his name is inscribed next to him. The Philistine, fallen on his knees, tries with a very lifelike gesture to ward off the blow; he is clad in a long tunic decorated with rows of small circles. This group is followed by two nimbed figures who stand side by side. The first, clad in the classical garb, holds a closed scroll. The second, considerably taller, wears a mantle fastened on the breast with a round brooch; he holds a long scroll with his name inscribed on it: the prophet Ezekiel. The three medallion portraits above this group have no accompanying inscriptions; the third portrait has been almost completely destroyed.

On the adjoining, slightly recessed wall we see two fighting cocks, and below this a man slaying a lion (fig. 43). The man is nude save for a short drapery tied above his left shoulder and barely covering his thighs; he holds a dagger in his left hand and with an awkward gesture attempts to behead the lion tamely seated in front of him. This group probably represents Samson killing the lion. The siren, carved on the lowest zone,[31] is now partly covered by grass, and only its head and the tip of its tail are visible.

Several animals are represented on the side wall of the niche: a camel, an eagle striking a hare, and two peacocks with intertwining necks, now partly hidden from view by grass (fig. 41). Farther to the right under the side window of the north exedra, we see two seated sheep, their heads turned backwards, and below them two standing figures (figs. 41, 46). The man on the left, identified by the inscription, is Hezekiah, the pious King of Judah who destroyed idolatry (II Kings 18). He is represented like an Oriental ruler: he wears a large turban, the ends of which come down in front over his shoulders; his richly embroidered coat is identical in shape and design with the one worn by Prince Hamazasp (figs. 44, 25). His face has been hacked off. Next to him stands the prophet Isaiah, also identified by an inscription; he is considerably taller than Hezekiah (fig. 45).

The story of the Fall is depicted on the front wall of the exedra (fig. 46). Adam and Eve stand on either side of the Tree of Life and are about to taste the fruit (fig. 47); their names are carved in large letters above their heads. To the right of the window is the badly damaged group of Eve and the serpent (fig. 48). Eve, kneeling, raises both hands and appears to be speaking or listening to the serpent, whose head almost touches hers. The serpent stands on four short legs and its body is partly coiled around the tree which is as large as the one in the preceding scene; some flowers of the lower branches are broken off. Eve's name is carved above her head.

Three cavalier saints, identified as St. Theodore, St. Sargis (Sergius), and St. George, are represented on the right face of the exedra and the adjoining recessed wall (figs. 49, 50). All three are nimbed, bareheaded, and clad in the classical military costume: a coat of armor over the tunic, and a short mantle tied on the right shoulder. Each one holds a long lance with a cross end, and with it stabs the animal or human figure trampled by the horse. Theodore kills a large serpent; the cross end of his lance is broken off (fig. 50). Sergius slays a panther (not visible on this photograph), and George a man whose hands and feet are fettered and who has fallen on his back (fig. 49). Three medallion portraits are represented above the cavalier saints: the first is identified as St. Cyriacus; no name accompanies the second youthful saint; the third is the prophet Hosea (figs. 49, 50).

On the polygonal walls of the northwest niche we see, in the first zone, the medallion portrait of a bearded saint. In the second zone two addorsed lions turn back their heads and look at a fox running above them; to the right is a large bear eating grapes (figs. 49, 51). In the lowest zone a young man, clad in a short tunic, pierces with his spear a lion reared on its hind legs and with one paw resting on a low pedestal; to the right a lion attacks a bull (figs. 49, 51). On this same niche, beyond the window, there is a quadruped and, under it, David killing the lion (fig. 52). David, clad in a close-fitting tunic and barefoot, is kneeling on one knee and he tears apart the jaws of the lion quietly standing in front of him. The inscription reads "the prophet David."

The stories of Daniel and of the Three Hebrew Children fill the west end of the north wall (Daniel 3.20–23, 6.16–23; fig. 49). The young Hebrews stand full-face, their hands raised in the attitude of prayer; the fiery furnace has not been represented. They wear short tunics and the Persian trousers or *anaxyrides* which fasten under their feet; their names, Hananiah, Mishael, and Azariah, are inscribed above their heads. Daniel in the den of lions stands in the same attitude as the three Hebrews; his tunic is slightly shorter, and over it he wears a large mantle fastened on the breast with a brooch. His name is inscribed above his head. The lions, standing on their front legs and with their bodies thrust vertically upward, lick Daniel's feet. Above the lion on the left, we see two half-length figures: an angel and a bearded man whom he has seized by the hair. The group is inspired by the apocryphal book of Bel and the Dragon. According to this story, when Daniel had been cast into the den, an angel appeared to the prophet Habakkuk and, commanding him to take with him the dinner he had just prepared, "laid hold of Habakkuk by the hair of his head and set him over the den in Babylon."[32] The medallion portrait to the right of Daniel represents the prophet Amos.

The left section of the vine scroll is badly damaged and only a few circumvolutions remain (fig. 40). Over the northeast niche we see: two confronted birds; a seated man holding a bunch of grapes and a large bird opposite him; a man digging with a spade which he pushes into the ground with his foot (figs. 40, 46). On the side wall of the north exedra two men, wearing only short trousers, are shown kicking each other; next, a man carrying a sling watches a large bird pecking at the grapes; this is followed by a seated ram eating grapes (figs. 41, 55). Turning the corner, to the front wall of the exedra, we see a large bird pecking at the grapes; followed by a man who carries a large basket on his shoulder and holds another in his left hand; next, a man stabs a bear who is trying to strangle him; a small bird pecks at the grapes (figs. 41, 53). On the right wall of the exedra and the adjoining recessed wall are represented two confronted birds and next to them two confronted goats standing on their hind legs; then, after a few circumvolutions which are not visible on the photographs, we see an animal standing on its hind legs and eating grapes, a human head above the vine branches, and a small quadruped running to the left (fig. 41). On the polygonal walls of the northwest niche a man is shown digging with a spade; a woman, carrying two large jars, walks toward him; next to her are two birds with a large pumpkin carved above the head of the second bird. The vine branches which separate to show a large bearded head are disposed in such a manner that they give the impression of representing the body and the outstretched arms of a man (fig. 54). On the end wall a man stands holding the vine branches and watching a bear reared on its hind legs; a man and his dog run toward this bear from the right (fig. 40).

Few of the animals, carved in high relief or in the round are sufficiently well preserved to be identified. To the right of the central window one can see three fish, one above another, then a stag head, a large bird, and a lion head (fig. 41).

ICONOGRAPHY AND STYLE

THE compositions and single figures depicted on the four façades may seem, at first sight, to have been selected at random, but a closer study shows that they are actually parts of a definite program which has both a general and a special meaning.

In a prominent position on the east façade appears the bust of Adam, the first figure of Christ according to the allegorical interpretation of the Old Testament, and the facial type of the father of mankind has intentionally been modeled on that of Christ. The words inscribed next to the medallion, "and Adam gave names to all the animals and wild beasts," explain the presence of the numerous animals carved in high or low relief. Moreover, the allusion to the garden of Eden reminds us that the Church itself is an image of paradise. We find here a somewhat different rendering of the paradisiacal garden frequently depicted on the pavement mosaics of Early Christian churches.[33] The garden itself, with its trees and flowers, is eliminated; only the animals remain, as on some ivories of the early centuries.

Paradise lost through the sin of our forefathers will be regained through the Incarnation, and John the Baptist, the last of the prophets and the first witness of Christ, is represented on this same façade in the characteristic pose of a man testifying. But John is "Elias which was for to come" and "is come already" (Matthew 11.14; 17.11–13). Therefore, Elijah stands opposite him in identical attitude and with the same facial type and costume. By showing the widow of Sarepta kneeling before the prophet an additional meaning is introduced, for Elijah sent to Sidon by the Lord is a figure of Christ, and the widow of Sarepta is symbolic of the church of the Gentiles which received Christ while the Synagogue did not recognize Him. This allegorical interpretation is based on the words of Jesus: "many widows were in Israel in the days of Elias . . . but unto none of them was Elias sent, save unto Sarepta, a city of Sidon, unto a woman that was a widow" (Luke 4.25–26).

The other figures of this eastern façade refer to the introduction and spread of Christianity in Armenia. Only one of them is clearly designated by an inscription, namely St. Gregory the Illuminator, who converted King Tiridates and thus established Christianity as the official religion of Armenia in the late third century, several years before the conversion of the Emperor Constantine. The two saints at the sides of the central window have usually been identified as the apostles Thaddeus and Bartholomew, who first brought the Gospel to Armenia. The saint on the left, clad in the traditional classical costume of the apostles, most probably represents Thaddeus, who preached in this southern region of Armenia, and whose legendary history shows definite connections with the Artzruni family. According to the historian Thomas Artzruni, when Thaddeus visited King Abgar of Edessa, "the great Artzruni prince, Khuran . . . was the first to believe in Jesus Christ and was baptized by Thaddeus."[34] The saint to the right of the window wears bishop's robes; the identification with the apostle Bartholomew is therefore questionable. I would suggest that he represents James, Bishop of Nisibis, a saint held in great veneration by the Armenian church and who, according to the Armenian tradition, was a cousin of Gregory the Illuminator. St. James had passed through the province of Vaspurakan on his way to Nisibis, he had miraculously caused a spring to gush forth, and his relics were preserved in the monastery dedicated to him and erected on the site of the miracle at Entzak'iar, on the southern shore of Lake Van.[35]

Again, because of special connections with this region and with the Artzrunis, we may identify as the apostle Thomas the saint depicted to the right of the bishop, beyond the wedge-shaped recess. According to the apocryphal Acts of Thomas, when his remains were brought to Armenia the Artzruni princes paid special honors to him and built a church where his relics were deposited.[36]

As a worthy descendant of these pious princes, King Gagik has erected the church which he presents to Christ "with proud faith," holding it "like a gold vase filled with manna, and like a gold casket filled with perfume." The cross held by the angels and those which are carved higher up on this west façade remind us that this church was dedicated to the Holy Cross.

The narrative compositions carved on the south and north façades illustrate episodes from the Old Testament. Several of these—the story of Jonah, the sacrifice of Isaac, David's fight against Goliath, the Three Hebrew Children in the fiery furnace, Daniel in the den of lions —belong to the Early Christian cycle of scenes inspired by the *commendatio animae*, the prayers commending to God the souls of the deceased. These paradigms of divine deliverance were no doubt intended to suggest that like the righteous men of former days, King Gagik "begging for the remission of his sins" would receive the reward he beseeched. Other scenes or single figures also stress the idea of divine assistance. Thus Samson killed the Philistine and a lion, and David also slew a lion, thanks to the strength given them by the Lord. Hezekiah, who abolished idolatry, appears as the model of the pious king. In his fight against the Assyrians he was helped by "the angel of the Lord," who smote "an hundred four-score and five thousand"; and his prayer was heard when he fell ill. Next to him stands the prophet Isaiah, through whom Hezekiah received the sign that the Lord would heal him (II Kings 18–20).

No Gospel scenes have been depicted but several of the single figures display the parallelism between the Old and the New Testament. The enthroned Christ and the Virgin occupy approximately the same place on the south façade that Adam and Eve occupy on the north façade; the Redemption is thus opposed to the Fall, for Christ is the "new Adam" and Mary, the instrument of the Incarnation, is the "second Eve." The cavalier saints Theodore, Sergius, and George, triumphing over the power of evil, are the Christian counterparts of the Biblical heroes. The Three Hebrew Children and Daniel, who were ready to suffer death for their faith at the hands of the King of Babylon, may be considered as distant prototypes of the two Artzruni princes, "martyrs and witnesses of Christ," killed by the Moslem rulers. The prominence given to these two in preference to more famous martyrs, once again brings to the fore the desire to connect the decoration with the history of the Artzruni family and to recall the role played by the Artzrunis as true defenders of the faith. The long years of Arab domination in Armenia and the religious persecutions which continued to be a serious menace even during this period of semi-independence gave a note of actuality to all these representations.

In a few instances we can see why certain medallion portraits were placed close to specific scenes. Thus Samuel, who anointed David, appears above him, and farther to the left we have the bust portrait of Eli, Samuel's teacher. Zephaniah may have been represented above the Jonah cycle because he predicted the destruction of Nineveh (2.13). But in other instances the guiding principle is not evident, especially as we do not always have an identifying inscription. Portraits of various prophets and saints have been carved on the façades, just as they were depicted in mosaics or paintings in Armenian and other churches. This method of transferring to the outer walls part of the inner decoration is not entirely an innovation. In the sixth-century church of Ptghni, in northern Armenia, the carvings on the archivolt of a window—the image of Christ in a medallion held by two angels and flanked by busts of saints in medallions— repeated the usual decoration of the arch around the apse.[37] The medallion portraits of Aght'amar are also ultimately derived from such models.

The decorative program of Aght'amar is an original creation; some of the elements go back to the Early Christian period but they have been combined with others and given a new meaning. The church is an image of paradise and the sculptures exalt the idea of the Redemption which has come through the Incarnation and the foundation of the Christian universe. The Gospel, carried to the four corners of the world by the evangelists, whose large figures, placed under the gables, dominate the four façades, was also preached in Armenia by one of the apostles, and Christianity was firmly established there by Gregory the Illuminator. The Artzrunis, the princely house of Vaspurakan, played a prominent role in the early history of the Church; their descendants continued to be the true defenders of the faith, and they and their people will receive the assistance and protection which God granted to the righteous men of the old covenant and to the servants of Christ.

The historian Ghevond, who lived in the middle of the eighth century, reports that the Arabs destroyed "the images of the true incarnation of our Lord and Saviour, and those of His disciples" wherever they saw them. Religious art suffered an eclipse during this period of Moslem domination, and when the country was freed it was natural that the artists should take as models the works produced before the Arab conquest in the middle of the seventh century. This explains, to a large degree, the use of early iconographic types in these sculptures of the medieval period. Several of the themes depicted at Aght'amar may be seen on the sepulchral stele or cross stones (*khatchk'ar*) and on the historiated capitals from old churches; for instance the Sacrifice of Isaac, Daniel in the den of lions, the Three Hebrews in the fiery furnace.[38] Samson killing the lion with his bare hands, the angel carrying the prophet Habbakuk through the air—part of the composition of Daniel in the den of lions—are carved on the façade of the seventh-century church of Ateni-Sion, in Georgia; the Armenian inscriptions which accompany these figures attest that they are the work of an Armenian sculptor.[39]

Other compositions, of which no earlier Armenian examples have been preserved or are known to date, also show the survival of old types. The story of Jonah is developed in several scenes, and Jonah and the boatmen are nude, as on the Christian sarcophagi, while contemporary and even earlier monuments of the Christian East represented them clothed. Our sculptor has even retained a characteristic detail, ultimately derived from Jewish apocrypha. According to these texts, "the intense heat in the belly of the fish had consumed Jonah's garments and made his hair fall out";[40] consequently, Jonah has his full hair when cast into the sea, but is completely bald after he has been ejected. The two episodes of Jonah's ejection by the whale and his rest under the gourd tree have been contracted and Jonah, depicted only once, lies opposite the monster whose jaws are wide open. But the sculptor of Aght'amar has developed the story of Jonah's preaching in Nineveh; the gestures of the men represented in medallions call to mind the decree of the King: "let man and beast be covered with sack-cloth, and cry mightily unto God" (Jonah 3.8). This is a novel interpretation, much more vivid than the mere grouping of the people before the gates of the city, as painted in some Byzantine manuscripts.[41]

An even more interesting departure from established iconographic types occurs in the group of Eve and the serpent, a composition which has no parallel in Christian art. Like the gifted artist of the Cathedral of Autun, who, two centuries later, carved the figure of Eve lying on the ground and probably listening to the serpent, the sculptor of Aght'amar has devised an original composition, much more compelling in the feeling of intimacy which it evokes, than the usual type of Eve standing next to the tree. In illustrating the temptation of Eve, the artists were faced with the problem of representing the serpent, before it was cursed to go on its belly, in a manner in which it would seem to be erect and yet close to its normal appearance. The solution usually adopted was to show the serpent coiled around the trunk of the tree; in the Byzantine Octateuchs we see a strange animal which has the form of a camel with a serpent along its back, a type inspired by a Jewish legend.[42] At Aght'amar the serpent walks on four legs, but as these legs are very short the normal appearance of the reptile has not been drastically modified.

Some of the New Testament figures also go back to very old models. Cavalier saints, frequently represented in Coptic art, appear as often and at a very early period on Armenian and Georgian monuments, probably independently of Coptic influence. For the image of the cavalier God was even more at home in Anatolia, where it had a long history. Some of these pagan divinities were represented spearing a serpent; witness the Greek coins of the first century B.C., from Isidia, in Lycia.[43] The group of the rider trampling or slaying an enemy has been widely used in different contexts: on Jewish or Christian amulets Solomon, on horseback, spears a prostrate female figure; on early Byzantine coins a barbarian is trampled by the horse of the triumphant emperor, and sometimes the barbarian is replaced by a serpent.[44] These types of triumph over the enemy or over the powers of evil were naturally adopted for the representations of cavalier saints. In Armenia we see an example as early as the sixth century on a fragmentary capital discovered on the site of Dvin, the ancient capital. A rider trampling a serpent coiled under the horse's hoofs occupies one side of the capital while on the other the medallion of Christ has been carved above the cross.[45] Two confronted riders, spearing serpents, were depicted on a slab from Ani.[46] In the seventh-century church of Lmbat cavalier saints were painted on either side of the apse.[47] To the two principal military saints, Theodore and George, the sculptor of Aght'amar has added the Armenian martyr Sargis or Sergius who, in the national tradition, became the defender par excellence against all kinds of evil and dangers. For, just before dying, he had begged God to protect all those who invoked Him in his name. "Grant to all those who believe in you and invoke my name for intercession, the remission of their sins, and save their souls and bodies from all dangers and the persecutions of the demons; grant health to the sick, victory to those who are in battle, release to those who are in captivity and prison, freedom to those who are in bondage," and so forth.[48] Theodore is represented transfixing a serpent in conformity with the early tradition, for the legend of George killing the serpent is of much later date. George is shown trampling a man who in some monuments is designated as the Emperor Diocletian.[49]

In only one instance does the composition depart both from the accepted types and the Biblical text: Samson instead of tearing the lion's jaws with both hands—"he rent him as he would have rent a kid and he had nothing in his hand" (Judges 14.6) —attempts to behead him with his dagger, and the lion who had "roared against him," is tamely seated in front of Samson.

Profane elements intermingle, here and there, with the religious scenes. The imaginary animals, such as the siren and the griffon, and the groups of confronted or fighting animals cannot be included in the representation of the paradisiacal garden, nor can the man spearing a lion be connected with a Biblical episode. But it is primarily in the animated scroll which girds the upper part of the church that the secular intrusion is most evident. The vine does not have here the symbolic meaning given to it in other Christian monuments; the crowned man drinking and eating fruit, seated in the middle of the scroll on the east façade, the other men hunting, wrestling, or tilling the soil, all these genre scenes show the enjoyment of the fruits of the earth and familiar episodes of daily life.

Some of these scenes recall the decorations of Gagik's palace at Aght'amar, mentioned above, which depicted the enthroned ruler, surrounded by young men, "attendants of his re-joicings"; groups of musicians and dancers; wrestlers and men with bared swords; lions and other wild animals and various species of birds. These themes belong to the typical cycle of palace decoration in Iranian and Islamic art. The Sasanian examples are known only through fragmentary remains. Painted stuccoes found at Ctesiphon show female dancers, musicians, and various animals, some of them running against a foliate background.[50] On the pavement mosaics of the courtyard or *iwan* of the palace of Shapur I at Bishapur we see again musicians, dancing girls, and courtesans.[51] A great diversity of scenes, some of them distributed around the central figure of the ruler, is preserved in the palaces and hunting lodges of the Umayyad caliphs at Qasr al Hayr al Gharbi, in Syria, and at Qusayr' Amra and Khirbet al Mafjar, in Jordan.[52] The fragmentary paintings from the capital of the Abbasid rulers, at Samarra, north of Baghdad, include hunting scenes, dancers, and acanthus scrolls with animal and human fig-ures.[53] King Gagik, who had visited the courts of the caliph and of the emir of Atropatene, may have seen similar examples and derived the inspiration for the general type of decoration which he used in his palace and in part on the church he erected.

The central section of the vine frieze on the east façade retains the principal elements of the banqueting scene familiar through the reliefs of Sasanian and post-Sasanian silver plates,[54] through later examples of Moslem art in ivory, metalwork, ceramics, textiles, and the frontis-pieces of manuscripts written for a king. The musicians and dancers who usually form part of these compositions have been omitted at Aght'amar, for obvious reasons, but the main figures remain: a king is seated cross-legged holding a wine glass, rather than the stemless cup favored by Moslem artists, and he is attended by two men wearing the costume of noblemen, namely, the tunic or the coat girded with a metal belt with pendants (fig. 39). Though the crown dif-fers from the one worn by Gagik on the west façade, it is probable that this image was also in-tended to represent the King.

The scenes which develop on the other façades of the church do not represent a royal hunt but rather rural scenes, for the only mounted figure, the rider shooting an arrow at a bear, is a later addition, as mentioned above in the description. Most of the men are peasants, clad in short tunics, and the episodes are scenes of their daily life. They hunt birds and hares; they wrestle with one another, or are more peacefully occupied, gathering grapes or tilling the soil. They defend themselves as best they can against wild animals, stabbing bears with their large knives, or using slings and sticks, even when faced by a lion. The nobles or older men, differentiated from the peasants by their long tunics, rest in the vine arbor or hunt bears with a bow and arrow.

These episodes of rural life depicted in the vine frieze are ultimately derived from the peopled scrolls which were so widely used during the Roman and Early Christian periods[55] and which also appear in Sasanian art. From Sasanian art, or more probably from the Early Christian examples in Syria, these compositions passed into Islamic art and were used in the decoration of the Umayyad palaces of the eighth century. On the fragmentary stucco reliefs from Khirbet al Mafjar, near Jericho, one can recognize many of the themes represented at Aght'amar: vintage, hunting, and pasturing scenes; a bear standing on its hind legs and eating grapes; men attacked by lions; beasts pursuing their prey.[56] Armenians had long been familiar with such representations, and a few examples which date from the period prior to the Arab conquest are preserved. A lintel, partly broken, discovered near Dvin, the ancient capital of Armenia, is decorated with a vintage scene.[57] Human figures and animals in vine scrolls were carved on large stone slabs which were later used in the construction of the church of Zvart'-nots, erected by the Catholicos Nerses III (641–661); on one of these a man faces a lion standing on its hind legs.[58] The style of the Aght'amar vine scroll is closer to that of Early Christian and especially of old Armenian examples, than it is to any of the Islamic monuments.

Human heads appear among the vine branches at Aght'amar, a few are included in the animal friezes under the eaves, and there are two uninterrupted rows of male and female heads under the eaves on the north and south walls of the west exedra (figs. 16, 40). These heads, which with two exceptions are shown in front view and are cut immediately above the neck, may well represent masks, though the theory that they copy actual masks used during the performances of a contemporary Armenian theater cannot be accepted, for it is based on a misinterpretation of the texts.[59] The motif is of Iranian origin. Severed heads, seen in frontal view, were used to decorate the Parthian palace of Hatra in the Mesopotamian Desert; similar heads have recently been discovered at Hamadan, the ancient Ecbatana, and at Qum, the holy city of Iran, south of Teheran.[60] According to some scholars they may have had originally an apotropaic character but by the classical period they had become an ornamental motif. A gold phial found at Panagurishte in Bulgaria is decorated with three concentric heads of Negro type;[61] aligned heads adorn several Coptic textiles and we see them at a much later period in Armenia, on the ceramics of the twelfth and thirteenth centuries found at Dvin and at Ani.[62]

The principal elements of the vine frieze, with the banqueting scene in the center, recall, as we have seen, the decoration of the Sasanian and Umayyad palaces; one would prob-ably have found as many analogies with Abbasid art if a greater part of the paintings of Sa-marra had been preserved. But what makes this connection particularly interesting is that at Aght'amar the palace cycle has been used for a church.

We know from literary sources and from surviving monuments that secular themes were sometimes depicted on the walls of Early Christian churches as well as on the pavement mosa-ics. For instance, at St. Costanza, in Rome, a Nilotic landscape encircled the base of the dome; a deer and a lion hunt are painted on the walls of one of the chapels at Bawit, in Egypt.[63] The Byzantine emperors of the Iconoclastic period are said to have added scenes of the hippodrome and of the hunt to the images of trees, plants, and birds, but after the triumph of the defenders of the Images in 843 all such representations disappear from Byzantine churches and the only secular themes, such as animals carved on the chancel screens, have a purely decorative func-tion.[64] This also characterized the earlier examples, with the possible exception of the subjects used by the Iconoclastic emperors; the motifs or scenes did not have a special meaning, they were not part of an iconographic program connected with the activities of the ruler.

That such a secular program could be developed at Aght'amar, alongside the religious scenes, and placed in a prominent position is due to the fact that the church was the royal chapel built close to the palace and had a gallery reserved for the King. Aght'amar is the oldest extant example of the combination of religious and secular themes adopted for a palatine church, but two monuments of later date, and in different countries, show that this was not an isolated case. At the Church of St. Sophia, in Kiev, the frescoes painted in the eleventh century on the walls of the staircases leading to the royal tribune represent performances at the hippo-drome in the presence of an emperor and an empress: acrobats, dancers, musicians, races, hunting scenes, and combats between men and beasts.[65] The art of Kievan Russia was influ-enced by that of Constantinople, and these compositions are related to Byzantine imperial iconography. Depicted close to the part of the building reserved for the ruler, they were visible only to him and to his attendants, but at the Cappella Palatina, in Palermo, the secular themes are introduced into the church itself. The mosaics which cover the walls of this church, built by Roger II between 1132 and 1140 and decorated during his reign and that of his successor William I, present an extensive cycle of Old and New Testament scenes, an array of saints and prophets based on Byzantine models. The rich decorations of the ceiling, painted in an Orien-tal style and perhaps by Moslem artists, depict festivity scenes.[66] A turbaned man, seated cross-legged, holding a wine cup and usually flanked by assistants, is represented more than once. There are also musicians, dancers, hunters; familiar scenes of everyday life; and a variety of real and imaginary animals.

In these two palatine churches, Aght'amar and the Cappella Palatina, erected by rulers who were in contact with the Arabs and familiar with their art, scenes from the palace cycle have been introduced into the decoration of the church. It is interesting to recall an example of similar usage in a church which was not a royal foundation, but which was within the Arab world. A large wooden screen, used as an iconostasis for one of the chapels in the triforium of the Coptic Church of Saint Barbara, in Old Cairo, is decorated with carved panels depicting a variety of scenes.[67] Some of them show the familiar groups of confronted or fighting animals in floral scrolls; others depict falconers, hunters on foot or on horseback fighting wild animals. In one of the larger panels we see a seated musician flanked by two men, and next to this group another seated figure who appears to be holding a cup and is waited on by two attendants. These reliefs, which have been dated in the late tenth century, are the work of Coptic sculptors, but they have marked affinities, both in style and subject matter, with the carved wooden panels from the palace of an Egyptian caliph of the Fatimid period. The decorations of the chancel screen of Saint Barbara, though inspired by the palace cycle, are comparable to the mythological scenes and animal figures used for purely ornamental purposes in Byzantine churches; the Cappella Palatina and Aght'amar are closer to one another by their general conception and intent.

In the Sicilian church, where the secular themes were painted in the high ceiling, and were not clearly visible from below, dancers, musicians, and genre scenes were not excluded; but the compositions are not centered around the image of a ruler, and consequently their connection with the royal founder is not as apparent as it is at Aght'amar. Here, Gagik, whose role and that of his forebears as true defenders of the Christian faith was stressed in the religious program set forth by the large figural frieze, also wished to appear in his secular role, enjoying the pleasures of peace and providing for his people the enjoyment of the fruits of the earth.

We mentioned previously that during the earlier centuries the sculptured decoration of Armenian churches had been restricted to specific areas, around the doors and windows, and that a blind arcade had sometimes been carved all around the church. The method used at Aght'amar, whereby the decoration extends to all parts of the building and includes, in particular, a wide frieze of figural sculpture, is characteristic of the art of the Near East, from a very early period on into the Middle Ages and even to the later centuries. Once again the Umayyad and Abbasid monuments, with their richly ornamented façades, may have been the immediate sources of inspiration. Similarities may even be noted in some specific features. For instance, at Khirbet al Mafjar friezes of partridges or of gazelles, sheep, and other beasts encircle the bases of the domes of the bath chamber and of the outer room,[68] just as at Aght'-amar animal friezes are carved under the eaves of the church and under the conical roof of the dome. But there are also significant differences between Aght'amar and the Moslem monuments. Whereas in the latter all available space is covered with stucco or stone carvings, at Aght'amar large areas are left bare and the component elements of the decoration are clearly separated from one another. More attention has also been paid, on the whole, to adapting this decoration to the architectural design. The composition of the west façade is the most successful, with the figures and large crosses symmetrically placed at the sides of the windows and triangular recesses. On the east the addition of a second bust figure on the right has slightly disturbed the harmonious grouping, but in spite of this one can note a definite attempt to balance the composition of the two end walls.

The south and north façades, with the projecting exedrae and the polygonal contours of the niches, presented greater problems. The front wall of the north exedra (the south is now hidden from view by the belfry) is again treated as a unit and the two Genesis scenes frame the central window, but elsewhere the sculptors have paid little attention to the projecting and retreating sections, and have treated these walls as if they presented a uniform surface. Thus in the group of the Virgin between angels, one angel is crowded into the narrow space to the left of the wall, while the other stands at a short distance, on the other face of the polygonal niche (fig. 21). This disregard for the shape of the surface is even more marked when a figure is carved on the two faces of a stone which forms an angle; such is the case with one of the addorsed lions on the north façade, or the lion standing on his hind legs just below (fig. 49). The medallions, carved for the most part on the third stone course above the palmette scroll, constitute the upper frame of the friezes, but within each frieze there is no uniformity in the size of the figures. Where two scenes are placed one above the other, as in the Jonah story (fig. 19), the figures are naturally much smaller; when there is no medallion or other ornament immediately above a figure, the figure is much taller than his neighbors, probably in order to maintain the overall height of the frieze. Only Goliath, and to a lesser degree Samson, project into the fourth stone course, in order to stress the fact that one was a giant and the other a very strong man. But there are also cases when differences in size cannot be explained, and the most striking example is that of the figure of Christ, on the west façade, shorter than that of Gagik instead of taller (fig. 5). This is obviously a mistake, a mistake which might have occurred because all the figures were carved before they were set in place. Perhaps to make this disparity in the sizes less obvious, the seraph on the right is of the same height as Christ, while the seraph on the left is of the same height as Gagik.

Several sculptors, some less skilled than others, were at work at Aght'amar; however, the traits common to the workshop are more marked than the individual differences. The figures stand out in fairly high relief from the background but there is hardly any surface modeling; deep grooves or shallow incisions delineate the features and the folds of the draperies. The bodies are seen in three-quarter or front view, with the weight evenly distributed on both legs; the feet are placed in profile or symmetrically turned outward, or occasionally one foot is in profile, the other slightly foreshortened. There is little movement even where action is indicated; only the gesture of the Philistine, warding off Samson's blow, introduces a realistic note into this series of hieratic images. The draperies are schematized; the overlapping folds are flattened as if they had been pressed with a hot iron. Sometimes the folds are carved in long, unbroken lines which roughly outline the shape of the leg; at other times the area between the folds is covered by a succession of curved lines creating a decorative pattern. In spite of the stylization and the static poses, many of these figures seem to be endowed with great vitality, due partly to the bold treatment and partly to the intense expression of the faces with their large, almond-shaped eyes.

There is very little connection between the figure style of these sculptures and the few examples of contemporary Islamic stucco or stone carvings which are known. The direct antecedents of Aght'amar are the seventh-century Armenian reliefs, some of which, like the enthroned Virgin and Child carved on the cross stones, or the lions standing on their front legs on either side of Daniel, show marked affinities with the representations of Aght'amar.[69] Religious art, except for illuminated manuscripts and liturgical objects produced in the privacy of the monasteries, had been at a standstill during the two centuries of Arab domination, and when churches could once again be erected and decorated, the sculptors naturally sought the earlier examples just as the architects themselves imitated, at first, the plans of older monuments. However, there must have been also a fresh influx of religious objects brought from the Byzantine empire, and it is possible that some of the sculptors of Aght'amar, who we are told came from different regions, had been working in neighboring countries where artistic activity had not been so drastically curtailed. For, in spite of significant differences, one can detect in these sculptures some knowledge of contemporary Byzantine art. Indications of this are a slightly better rendering of the human figure, a closer approximation of the general scheme of the classical himation, an attempt to differentiate between the smooth and pleated areas of the draperies instead of covering them uniformly with parallel lines.

The iconographic type of Gagik offering a model of the church to Christ also suggests a knowledge of Byzantine models, or of works which imitated them, for although the type itself goes back to a very early period, it was more widely used from the ninth century on.[70] In earlier Armenian monuments different types of the portraits of founders are to be seen. On the sixth-century church of Ptghni the founder, Manuel Amatuni, is represented killing a lion, a composition derived from the portraits of Sasanian rulers. In the following century, at Mren, the founders advance, in respectful attitude, toward the central figure of Christ flanked by saints, an iconographic type which may be seen on the apse mosaics of Early Christian churches where the founder is introduced by saints to Christ or to the Virgin. Beginning with Aght'amar, we find almost invariably in Armenia the donor holding the model of the church.[71]

The Artzruni historian speaks of this image of Gagik as being "a true likeness"; elsewhere in the text he is described as a tall man, of radiant appearance, with black arched eyebrows, dark wavy hair falling in thick locks from his lofty brow, and a downy beard which covered his ruddy cheeks.[72] Despite its damaged condition, the face does have a lifelike quality and one feels that there has been some attempt at portraiture; we can at any rate be sure that the details of the costume have been accurately rendered. This is of particular importance, for the kings of Vaspurakan did not strike coins and the relief of Aght'amar is our only contemporary visual document.

The crown worn by Gagik is probably the one given to him by the Emir Yusuf, which, as previously mentioned, was of pure gold of an intricate design, enriched with pearls and other costly jewels (figs. 7, 9). Though the relief is badly damaged, we can see that it had winglike motifs at the sides, recalling one of the types of Sasanian crowns. A greatly simplified form of the Sasanian crown may be seen on two monuments of the Umayyad period. The headdress of the ruler who was represented on the center of the façade at the palace of Qasr al Hayr al

Gharbi consists of a skull cap with a circular band from which rise a pair of wings framing a large jewel; a graffitto on the palace of Mshatta depicts a man with the same type of crown. The crown worn by the ruler on a post-Sasanian silver plate at the Hermitage Museum, in Leningrad, follows the same general model: a pair of wings, treated like palmette leaves, rise from the semicircular motif at the sides, while the central motif is surmounted by a crescent.[73]

The Abbasid caliphs did not wear crowns; their headdress had the shape of a round cap with two ribbonlike bands hanging at the sides, as can be seen from the portraits of al Muta-wakkil on a silver coin dated A.H. 241 (A.D. 855) and that of al Muqtadir (908–932), a contemporary of Gagik, stamped on a medallion.[74] But other Moslem rulers of this period are occasionally represented wearing the winged crown. On a silver medal found at Nishapur, in eastern Iran, the sovereign seated cross-legged between two attendants wears a crown "com-posed of two rows of pearls around the forehead, fastened with a ribbon on the left, supporting two half-palmettes on each side of a crescent and two stones."[75] The wings are more prominent on the crown worn by the Buyid prince 'Adud al-Dawlah, whose portrait adorns both sides of a gold medal minted at Fars in A.H. 359 (A.D. 970); the large wings, outlined by a pearled border, frame a central rosette and a crescent.[76]

These examples prove that, though not worn by the Abbasid caliphs themselves, a winged crown, a distant descendant of the Sasanian type, was still in use during the ninth and tenth centuries and we have, therefore, very good reason for accepting the crown worn by Gagik on the Aght'amar relief as a faithful copy of the one he had received from the Emir Yusuf. The tunic and mantle fashioned in richly embroidered or woven materials (fig. 7) are also probably the royal robes given to Gagik at the time of his coronation, although the Artzruni historian mentions only the tunic. The design of interlocking circles is ultimately derived from Sasanian textiles, and the birds enclosed in these circles recall the materials represented on the Sasanian reliefs of Taq-i-Bustan.

The garments worn by the two Artzruni princes and by Saul and Hezekiah, depicted as Oriental rulers, as well as the tunic of the Philistine killed by Samson, may show the types of materials woven in Armenia (figs. 24–26, 42, 44). We know that the textile industry was highly developed in Armenia. The Arab writers frequently mention the carpets and the woolen and silk fabrics which were greatly valued, especially those which were dyed with the *kirmiz*, an aphis found in the spring on the roots of a plant growing on the slopes of Mount Ararat. As an example of the appreciation and of the good quality of these materials, one may recall the account of the reception of a Byzantine ambassador in 917 at the court of al Muqtadir. Wishing to impress his guest the caliph had hung in his palace 38,000 curtains of which 12,000 were of gold brocade. The Arab author who describes this rich display has listed the country of origin of the different cloths, and the Armenian materials are among the first to be mentioned.[77] Armenian historians also refer to the various types of fabrics made in their coun-try, the rich garments worn by the princes or sent as presents, for instance the robes with gold ornaments and the rugs with figured designs woven by the women of Armenia.[78] Thus, while

Gagik's mantle is in all probability the one given by the caliph or the Emir Yusuf, the other garments may show the designs of materials manufactured in Armenia as well as the style of dress worn in the tenth century. The nobles followed the Arab fashions, but I have not been able to find exact parallels for most of the costumes among the few known Moslem examples of the ninth and tenth centuries. The Artzruni prince Sahak and Saul both wear a kind of long coat which crosses diagonally from left to right and is held at the waist by a belt with three pendants, probably made of leather and studded with metal plaques (figs. 24, 26). Sahak's tunic, seen at the opening of the neck, is plain while that of Saul has an embroidered collar. The type of belt seen in these reliefs is probably of Central Asiatic origin; its use spread widely among other peoples beginning with the late sixth century. We see it at Taq-i-Bustan and on some silver plates which may be post-Sasanian; in Georgia, in the early seventh century, on the image of the prince carved on the west façade of the Church of the Holy Cross, at Djvari; and in Islamic art in the ninth century and later.[79] The pendants of the belt worn by the hunts-man represented on a ninth-century wall painting at Nishapur are much longer than ours, and grouped together in front, but in the paintings from Samarra, the city founded by the Abbasids in 836 and abandoned in 892, we see exactly the same type of belt as at Aght'amar.[80]

The garment worn by the other Artzruni prince, Hamazasp, and by Hezekiah is slit in front, below the knees, like Gagik's tunic, but it has lapels like a coat (figs. 25, 44). The lapeled coat, also of Central Asiatic origin, was adopted by the Arabs, but in all the examples hitherto known, in the paintings of Chinese Turkestan as well as in Islamic monuments, this coat is always worn with a belt, and the lapel is of the same material as the coat, instead of being made of a different material as it is at Aght'amar.[81] The Central Asiatic and Islamic type may be seen at Aght'amar in the vine frieze, on the figure to the right of the seated king; his companion wears a simple tunic, but also girt with the belt with three pendants (fig. 39).

Many of the animals carved under the eaves or enclosed in the vine frieze, and some of the larger animals represented below, are treated in a fairly naturalistic manner. The movement of the bull which a boy has seized by the horns is well observed, so is that of the hind with a suckling fawn who bends her head to bite her leg (fig. 17). The running animals are sometimes depicted in the conventional attitude of the "flying gallop," but we also see a more natural position of the legs. At times the faces of these animals show a good deal of expression, for instance, the bear which devours the grapes with such voracity (fig. 51). Side by side with these natural forms we see, especially in the lower parts of the façades, legendary animals, confronted, addorsed, and fighting beasts, birds with intertwined necks, in fact, most of the old Mesopotamian motives which had passed into Sasanian art and spread to the neighboring countries of Asia, to Byzantium, and farther west in Europe. The ultimate derivation from Sasanian art is apparent at Aght'amar in many of the individual forms as well as in specific details, such as the bands around the necks, wings, and tails of the birds, or the palmettes which mark the upper parts of the wings of these birds or of the legs of the quadrupeds (figs. 28, 29). The detailed ornamental treatment of the surfaces and the type of stylization point to the imitation of textiles, but the immediate models were probably not Sasanian works. It is true that in Sasanian textiles as well as stuccoes one can see the beaded bands on the neck or wings of various animals, but these bands do not encircle the body as they do on the griffon and the bird with horned head at Aght'amar. Parallel examples occur, however, in Islamic textiles which are derived from the Sasanian. On the fragmentary silk with Kufic inscriptions from the Treasury of St. Servatius, in Maastricht, the beaded band woven across the chest of the lion also runs along the sides of the neck.[82] The direct sources of inspiration must therefore have been contemporary fabrics rather than century-old examples. In the present state of our knowledge it is impossible to tell whether those contemporary fabrics were Islamic or Armenian products. We have ample evidence that Islamic textiles were sent to Armenia, as gifts to the princes and other dignitaries, the Arabs following in this the practice of the Sasanian kings. We also know that different types of textiles, some with figured representations, were woven or embroidered in Armenia. Several fragments have been found in the excavations of Dvin and Ani, the ancient and medieval capitals of Armenia.[83] A larger and finer piece is preserved in the binding of an Armenian manuscript in the library of Erevan.[84] The rich design of this textile consists of roundels enclosing confronted birds at the sides of a conventionalized tree; the wide bands of the roundels are themselves decorated with four pairs of confronted peacocks separated by floral motifs. Beaded discs, surrounded by large pine cones, fill the lozenge-shaped spaces between the roundels. For our present study the question whether these textiles are local products or imports is less important than the fact that such textiles were known in Armenia and influenced the style of some of the animal figures carved at Aght'amar.

The sculptors of Aght'amar sometimes modified the forms they imitated. The second image of the whale in the Jonah story (fig. 19) is derived from the Persian senmurv or hippocamp frequently reproduced on Islamic and Byzantine textiles; the forepart of the animal, with the banded wing, the palmette above the leg, and the roundel on the articulation, faithfully depicts the form of this legendary beast, but its rear part, instead of ending in a peacock's tail, is a coiled fish tail like that of the sea monster on the sarcophagi of the Early Christian period. In Sasanian and post-Sasanian art ribbons are sometimes tied around the legs of an animal; instead of these the sculptor of Aght'amar has represented in one instance the balls which falconers always tied to a hawk's legs (fig. 29). Accurate detail is here combined with a purely imaginary form.

The plant forms are limited to the grape vine, the palmette, and the pomegranate. The vine frieze which girds the church is rendered with a fair degree of naturalism and freedom. The leaves are transformed into rosettelike shapes but the branches from which hang the heavy clusters of grapes retain their plastic form and are not arranged in a regular pattern. They wind and curve following the design of a scroll or they spread over two or three figures; they are broken off to make room for a small group, or for a stem with interlacing branches; occasionally the vine is replaced by a pomegranate or a palm tree. This variety in the design animates the frieze and differentiates it from the Coptic or Islamic scrolls with their regular and often monotonous repetition. The palmette scrolls which cover the arches above the windows show a wide range of variations. Except for the undulating stems with half palmettes regularly filling the curves, carved on the intrados and extrados of the arches and of the palmette scroll, the same motif is hardly ever repeated more than twice. The following combinations have been used: upright full palmettes with interlacing stems (fig. 30); full palmettes in interlocking or interweaving circles (fig. 41, lower window, and fig. 32); an undulating stem with half palmettes in an almost vertical position which join to form a full palmette at the crown of the arch; half palmettes, without stems, which form a zig-zag motif and have smaller leaves in the triangular spaces (fig. 41, two windows of the drum); an undulating stem with half palmettes which make a double curve and have a cone-shaped offshoot (fig. 11); interweaving undulating stems with full palmettes and bunches of grapes alternately placed in the circles (fig. 17); half palmettes and bunches of grapes alternating at the sides of an undulating stem (fig. 34) or of a rigid stem (fig. 33). The wide lower frieze around the church is decorated with split palmettes enclosing bunches of grapes; these split palmettes are lodged in the circles formed by two undulating stems and there are pine cones between the circles. On the arch over one of the drum windows a row of birds takes the place of the foliate ornament. This marked interest in variety is characteristic of Armenian sculpture; on older monuments, such as Ptghni, a different motif is carved on each one of the arches which crown the windows.

The arches above the wedge-shaped recesses are decorated with pomegranate trees. This is a most unusual device, for a tree cannot easily be adapted to a narrow curved surface, and the common practice has always been to select for such an area a foliate motif or a simple geometric ornament. At Aght'amar the trunk of the tree is sharply bent at the angle formed by the arch and the horizontal band, and the general design, with alternating leaves and fruits symmetrically placed at the sides of the main branch and turning back, recalls the scheme used on one of the smaller arches (figs. 13, 14, 37, 39; compare with fig. 33). This simplified treatment of a tree or treelike motif, consisting of a vertical stem bearing alternately vine leaves and bunches of grapes, or made up of a succession of fanciful and varied ornaments springing from a vase, occurs elsewhere on narrow strips, for instance, at the Dome of the Rock in Jerusalem on the bronze plates which cover the tie beams or the lintels, and at Khirbet al Mafjar on the posts of the balustrades.[85] Earlier examples occur in Armenia. The arches on the façades of the seventh-century church of T'alin are decorated with pomegranate trees: small branches, each ending in a fruit, project diagonally on either side of the rigid stem; the root is slightly rounded.[86] The conical base of the Aght'amar trees may be seen on a torus moulding at Bishapur, decorated with a vine branch which ends in a large leaf like the pomegranate trees of Aght'amar; an earlier and more naturalistic type of the conical base is to be found at Palmyra.[87]

In all the arch decorations of Aght'amar the motifs stand out clearly against the shadows of the hollowed background. The palmette is the principal element and all the variations which have been noted above can be traced back to Sasanian art where this ornamental style, based on earlier forms, was first developed and had a wide distribution in the following centuries. But whereas in the Abbasid art of the ninth and tenth centuries the palmette and vine lost their original aspect and were transformed into abstract ornaments, at Aght'amar the earlier forms were perpetuated. Through the greater naturalism of individual elements or compositions, the foliate ornaments of Aght'amar differ entirely from those of contemporary Moslem art and are closer to the types used by Byzantine artists during this period. We need not, however, assume a direct connection with the Byzantines; in both instances the survival of the late classical tradition and a greater regard for natural forms prevented the extreme simplification which resulted elsewhere in pure abstractions.

By attempting to trace the origin of the various subjects or decorative motifs, and to find the immediate models or sources of inspiration, I do not wish to convey the impression that the sculptures of Aght'amar present a juxtaposition of various foreign elements. One would doubtless have found a greater number of parallel examples in Armenian art if so many of the monuments had not been destroyed. Even those elements which are ultimately derived from other sources have been modified in accordance with the national artistic trend, and the result is a unique monument which differs as much from the Islamic edifices as it does from contemporary or earlier Christian churches.

THE PAINTINGS

DESCRIPTION THE paintings which cover the interior walls of the church, have attracted little attention. Earlier publications mention, in passing, a few Gospel scenes; a general view of the south exedra and reproductions of three compositions in the west exedra have hitherto been the only available documents.[88] Thanks to the detailed new photographs the entire decoration can now be studied for the first time.

These paintings are contemporary with the sculpture; one need only confront some of the single figures with the corresponding reliefs to note the marked stylistic affinities. If we compare, for instance, any one of the bishops' portraits with the bishops carved on the east façade (figs. 34, 35, 60) we see the same thick-set frontal figures shown in bold outline; the same manner of stylization in the delineation of the draperies; the same facial types with a low, broad forehead and large, almond-shaped eyes; the same treatment of the mustache and beard, which encircle, as it were, the mouth. The angel of the Annunciation, with one wing sharply bent back in a horizontal line above his head, closely resembles the angel standing next to Christ on the south façade, and the throne of the Virgin is almost identical with her throne carved on this same façade (figs. 17, 21, 63). These and parallel examples leave no room for doubt that the paintings and sculptures are works of the same artistic school.

Contrary to the opinion advanced earlier by some scholars, it is now well established that there was no official opposition in Armenia to the representation of sacred subjects and that the churches were frequently adorned with an extensive Christological cycle.[89] The remains of mosaics and wall paintings have corroborated the evidence furnished by literary and historical sources. Some of these examples go back to the seventh century; for instance, in the church of Lmbat part of the apse decoration is still visible: an enthroned Christ is flanked by the wheels and the "living creatures" of Ezekiel's vision, each "creature" having four heads, those of a man, a lion, an ox, and an eagle. On the sides of the apse are two cavalier saints.[90] Fragmentary remains of Ezekiel's vision can also be seen in the apse of the church of T'alin. At T'alish Christ, holding a long scroll, decorated the conch of the apse while standing apostles were depicted on the side walls of the bema. In the church of Tat'ev, built in 930, the enthroned Christ again appears in the apse, and a grandiose composition of the Resurrection of the Dead covers the west wall. But only at Aght'amar have the paintings survived almost in their entirety, and the significance of this ensemble becomes even greater when we recall the scarcity of surviving monuments from this period in the Byzantine Empire and neighboring countries. Except for the rock-cut chapels of Cappadocia, the oldest of which can be assigned to the tenth century, there is no church earlier than the eleventh century which has retained its entire decoration. Thus, the paintings of Aght'amar, though partly damaged and repainted, and less impressive at first sight than the carvings on the outer walls, are of primary importance for the history of East Christian church decoration.

The most interesting fact revealed by these new photographs is the existence of paintings in the drum of the dome. Floral and geometric designs and confronted birds cover the conches of the small niches which alternate with the windows. Figure representations fill the upper half of the drum, and occasionally extend into the space between the niches and the windows (figs. 57, 58). More than a third of this decoration has disappeared, but it is evident from what remains that the story of Adam and Eve was originally painted all around the drum.

The cycle begins on the east, above the apse (fig. 58). A draped figure can be discerned to the left of the central window (extreme left on the photograph), and, to the right, one can clearly see a nude man standing full-face; the subject is, therefore, the creation of Adam, or rather Adam introduced into the Garden of Eden. The creation of Eve is represented in the space between the next two niches. The Creator, a large draped figure, bends forward and touches the right hand of Eve, whose bust, presented in front view and with raised arms, emerges from the side of Adam lying prone on the ground; a tree is drawn in the background, to the left of Eve. Part of a draped form may be seen in the next space, beyond the niche; judging from the direction of the folds, this figure is turned toward the scene of the creation of Eve, but the fragmentary condition of the painting does not allow a definite identification.

The paint has fallen off in the section of the drum which extends from this point to the northwest pendentive. Here, to the left of the window, the upper half of the Creator's figure can again be recognized; with raised hand, He addresses Adam and Eve, who stand in the next space, separated from Him by a large tree painted above the window (fig. 57, lower left corner). Adam and Eve are nude, save for a garland of leaves around their waists; the composition therefore represents Adam and Eve hiding from God after the Fall. An ornament, resembling a tree, separates this scene from the Expulsion depicted above the north exedra. An angel fills the space to the left of the window; he bends forward and appears to be pushing Adam and Eve, represented to the right of the window. In the adjoining space, beyond the niches and to the left of the window over the northeast pendentive, we see the large figure of a cherub who, sword in hand, guards the entrance of the Garden of Eden. There are some indistinct traces of painting in the next section, which adjoins the first scene described above.

The cycle began, therefore, with the introduction of Adam into the Garden of Eden and continued to the Expulsion. The parts now destroyed must have included some of the usual episodes of Genesis, such as: God presenting Eve to Adam; Eve tempted by the serpent; Adam and Eve tasting of the fruit of the tree. We have no way of knowing whether earlier moments of the Creation, or any other scenes or figures were represented in the dome before it was destroyed, a destruction which, as previously noted, did not affect the drum.

Faint traces suggest that the pendentives, the vaults, and the conches of the exedrae were also decorated, but only the paintings which begin below the level of the cornices have survived. Portraits of bishops are painted on three zones, one above another, in the diagonal niches and on the outer faces of the pilasters; interlacing floral designs cover the angular walls formed by these pilasters and the exedrae and niches (figs. 59–61, 66). Scenes from the Gospels are represented in the remaining parts of the church, namely in the four exedrae and on the piers which support the barrel vault in front of the west exedra.

A uniform layer of paint now covers the upper half of the apse and the piers in front of it, and the only remaining figures of the original decoration are the six apostles painted at the sides of the window (figs. 61, 62); the other six were no doubt represented on the inner faces of the two piers, three on each side. Some of the apostles hold the book of the Gospels, others a scroll as well as the book, which is then awkwardly placed above the left arm. The facial types, as well as the inscriptions which can be deciphered, help us to recognize Peter, standing to the left of the window, and Paul, Andrew, and Philip to the right.

The Gospel cycle begins in the upper zone of the south exedra, and the scenes follow one another in chronological order, but without any marked separation between them, along the upper zone of the west and north exedrae. There are no paintings in the second zone of the south exedra, which was occupied by the king's gallery; the narrative is resumed in the second zone of the west and north exedrae, it continued in a third zone but these paintings have almost entirely disappeared. A wide band, decorated with a double row of a pleated ribbon motif, separates the first and second zones of painting from one another, but only a narrow line is drawn between the second and third zones (fig. 64). The scenes are as follows, proceeding from left to right in each exedra.

South exedra, first zone: Annunciation (fig. 63). The angel advances from the left; Mary, with arms raised in the attitude of an *orans* figure, is seated full-face on an ornate throne which has a high back, slightly curved at the top. *Visitation* (fig. 63). Mary and Elizabeth clasp one another in a close embrace; their faces are turned toward the spectator. *Nativity* (fig. 59). Mary and Joseph are seated on either side of the manger, which is a high masonry structure placed under the arched opening of the cave; the infant Jesus lies on top of the manger, and the heads of the ox and the ass can be seen behind it. Two shepherds, wearing short tunics, close-fitting trousers, and pointed bonnets, stand behind Mary; a sheep (or a dog?) lies on the ground. The Magi, identified by an inscription, stand in a corresponding position on the right, behind Joseph.

West exedra, first zone: The composition on the pier before the exedra, to the left, is badly damaged. Three persons appear to be standing behind a table covered with a cloth; the sequence of the narrative suggests that the *Presentation of Christ in the temple* was painted here. *Joseph's dream* (fig. 64). The angel flies down toward Joseph, who lies on a mattress, his head resting on his right hand; the pillow has a checkerboard design. *Flight into Egypt* (fig. 64). Mary, holding the infant Jesus, is seated front view on the ass; Joseph, wearing a long mantle over his tunic, leads the way holding the bridle of the ass; a young boy follows, carrying a long staff and wearing a mantle attached to the left shoulder. Joseph's name is inscribed next to him. The ass seems to have been repainted. *Massacre of the innocents* (figs. 65, 66). The composition is divided into two parts. In the upper zone of the exedra Herod, crowned and nimbed, clad in a long tunic and chlamys, is seated on a high, ornate throne which has no back. A tall soldier, also crowned, stands in front of him; the soldier has seized a nude child by the ankles and raises his sword in order to kill him; the empty scabbard hangs from his belt. This figure seems to have been retouched and the crown may be the restorer's substitution for a helmet. Signs of repainting also appear in the space between Herod and the soldier. A nude child, lying on the ground, partly covers three smaller figures who stand in the background, turned toward the soldier; in the foreground are four nude figures turned toward Herod. Another nude child, standing behind the soldier, is turned to the right, and faces the part of the composition which continues on the pier before the exedra; here, six mothers standing in two rows watch the massacre in sorrowful but dignified attitudes (fig. 66).

North exedra, first zone: Baptism (figs. 60, 67). John stands in front of a tree and lays his hand on Christ's head; two angels stand on the right. The water comes up to Christ's armpits, and rays descend on His head. *Transfiguration* (fig. 67). Christ, holding the book raised in His left hand, stands in a pointed oval mandorla formed by four concentric bands and crossed by radiating lines; Moses, holding the tables of the law, is on the right; Elijah is on the left. Three apostles are represented in the foreground, in front of rocky hillocks: Peter, on the left, gazes at the vision, James and John, on the right, turn their backs to it. *Wedding feast at Cana* (fig. 67). Christ and several guests are seated around the table in the upper part of the picture; two servants, bearing cups, stand behind Christ. The window cuts into the lower part of the composition. On the left, the master of the feast watches the servant who is pouring water into a large basin; on the right two young men, one of whom is crowned, are seated cross-legged on the ground holding wine glasses in their hands (see also fig. 61, upper left).

West exedra, second zone: Christ teaching (?) The scene painted on the pier before the exedra, to the left, is badly preserved; Christ, standing on the right, appears to be addressing several persons grouped on the left. *Raising of Lazarus* (figs. 64, 68). Christ, followed by the apostles aligned in three rows one above another, stands next to the sepulcher which is merely suggested by a rectangular band drawn around the shrouded figure of Lazarus. Mary and Martha stand behind the sepulcher; their names are inscribed next to them. *Entry into Jerusalem* (figs. 64, 68). Christ, seated front view on the ass, approaches from the left, followed by the same compact group of apostles; five children spread their garments under the ass's feet. The roof of a rectangular building may be seen in the background, and, to the right, the head of Zacchaeus, who has climbed a palm tree. *Christ anointed at Bethany* (fig. 65). The painter has followed the account in the Gospel of John, 12.1–8. The large figure of Christ dominates the composition; Martha, identified by the inscription, approaches from the left, to serve Him, and Mary, standing in the foreground, holds His feet. The apostles are grouped on the right and only one person sits opposite Christ; this is probably Lazarus, who "sat at the table with Him." The man standing in the foreground may represent Judas, his gesture suggesting his protest against the waste of the costly ointment. A colonnaded building, with a small lamp hanging under the arches, fills the background. *Washing of the apostles' feet* (fig. 65). Christ holds Peter's legs with His left hand and raises the right in the gesture of speech; the towel hangs from His waist. Peter is seated on a faldstool; his feet barely touch a large basin and he raises his right hand to his head, in the characteristic gesture which illustrates his words: "Lord, not my feet only, but also my hands and my head" (John 13.9). Six apostles are grouped on the left, in front of a rectangular building; four others stand behind Peter, under a ciborium. *Christ before Pilate* (fig. 60). On the pier before the exedra, to the right, one can see Pilate, crowned, seated on a high throne placed under a ciborium; Christ and one other person stand before him.

North exedra, second zone: Crucifixion (figs. 67, 69). The top of the large wooden cross and part of Christ's nimb project into the ornamental band. Christ wears the long sleeveless garment, the *colobium;* His body is still erect but His head is slightly inclined and His eyes are closed. A semicircular band, suggesting the arc of heaven, frames His head, and two medallions, enclosing the personifications of the sun and the moon, are painted on either side of it. The two robbers are drawn on a smaller scale; their hands are tied behind their backs and they are nude, save for short skirts. The lance bearer pierces Christ's right side; he wears a long tunic, a chlamys, and a helmet; his left knee is sharply bent for his left foot rests on a higher level of the ground than the right one. The sponge bearer, on the other side of the cross, raises the sponge tied to a long staff; he wears a short tunic, and the bowl of vinegar is placed on the ground next to him. The Virgin, the apostle John, and one of the holy women stand at the sides of the rocky mount on which the cross has been raised. *The holy women at the sepulcher* (figs. 67, 69). The angel is seated front view on the left; his large wings, rising vertically, join at the tips and form a heart-shaped motif behind his head. The sepulcher has a pyramidal roof, divided into three horizontal bands; it is framed by an acanthus scroll at the base and half-acanthus leaves at the sides. The architrave rests on two large columns; the lunette has a diaper design, and the same motif, imitating grill work, covers the façade on either side of the arched door. A large rectangular stone is placed in front of the sepulcher, and it is covered with a cloth decorated with three crosses. Two holy women address the angel; the apostles John and Peter, identified by the inscription, stand higher up, in the background. *Harrowing of hell* (figs. 61, 67). Christ, holding the large double cross and accompanied by two angels, walks toward the right and bends slightly to seize Adam's hand. The painting is badly preserved. Above Adam and Eve one can barely see two rows of heads; these must represent the prophets and kings usually included in this scene. *Christ appearing to Mary Magdalene* (fig. 61). Christ stands on the right, turned to the left; His extended arms are covered by the ample folds of his mantle. Mary Magdalene kneels at His feet; only half of her figure is preserved. Behind her one can faintly discern a bearded man who stands facing Christ and raises both hands. A long inscription in vertical lines accompanies this scene; this is the only inscription in the church except for mere names. The letters above Christ's head and the last vertical line can easily be read, they are "Jesus Christ arisen" (*harutsial*). In the first line the word "with faith" (*havatov*) is clear, the following word seems to be "remember" (*hishea*). Only a few letters of the second line can be deciphered; the three letters in the small space between Christ's nimb and His right shoulder are GAG; a few other letters, which are quite blurred, are written above His nimb, on the left. This inscription must refer to the standing figure and I believe he represented King Gagik the beginning of whose name is preserved in these three letters, GAG.

The compositions of the third zone have almost entirely disappeared. In the west exedra, immediately under the Entry of Christ into Jerusalem and the left half of the Raising of Lazarus, the upper part of the *Ascension* still remains: Christ seated in a mandorla and borne by four flying angels.[91] There are faint traces of nimbed figures in the right half of the west exedra; these probably belong to the scene of *Pentecost*, for the Early Christian iconographic type of standing apostles, known through the Syriac Gospel of Rabula, survived in some Armenian manuscripts, even as late as the end of the thirteenth century. On the extreme right of the north exedra, where the last scene of the cycle would have been represented, we see part of a building and the head of a woman looking out of the window (fig. 61). The composition of the *Dormition of the Virgin* often includes two buildings, one at each end, and several women, the companions of Mary, look out from the windows.[92] It is probable that the fragmentary remain is part of the *Dormition*.

The last composition to be considered fills the conch above the south door (figs. 59, 70). The original representation is partly hidden by one or possibly two layers of overpaintings. These consist of a large bust of Christ, on the left; two nimbed heads and four large wings in the center; and part of a building on the right. However, one can still distinguish the main elements of the first layer. Christ, in a mandorla, occupies the uppermost section of the conch: below Him are two rows of thirteen (or fifteen?) nimbed figures. The men in the upper row are seen almost to their knees, they are clad in simple tunics and stand with crossed hands; the men in the second row are drawn full length. In the present state of preservation, one cannot tell whether other figures had been painted further down at the sides of the door. This composition, which will be discussed later, represents the Resurrection of the Dead or the *Second Coming of Christ*.

ICONOGRAPHY
AND STYLE

THE Genesis cycle painted in the upper zone of the drum is comparable to a continuous frieze at the base of a dome. This method of decoration goes back to late Antiquity and continued in use during the Early Christian period. At the Church of St. Costanza, in Rome, a Nilotic scene girded the base of the dome, and Biblical subjects were represented above it, in the spaces framed by caryatids rising from acanthus shrubs. In the dome of the Mausoleum of Cencelles (Tarragona), in Spain, hunting episodes follow one another, in an uninterrupted frieze, at the base of the dome, and Old Testament scenes, separated by columns, occupy the upper zones. In the fifth-century funerary chapel of El Bagawat, in Egypt, a continuous ring of Old Testament scenes, to which are added a few figures of saints and personifications, fills the greater part of the dome.[93] This decorative system re-emerges in Western Europe in the twelfth and especially the thirteenth centuries, and it is also adopted by some Byzantine artists of the Palaeologan period.[94] The most interesting Western examples, for our present study, are the thirteenth-century mosaics in the narthex of San Marco, in Venice, since they also depict the Genesis cycle in a dome, but the paintings of Aght'amar antedate them by three centuries.

In a letter, frequently cited by art historians, St. Nilus, who lived in the fourth century, recommended that Old and New Testament scenes, disposed in chronological order, be represented on opposite walls of the church. This system prevailed in Western Europe, but it is not known through any surviving monuments of the East Christian world, where preference was given to the Christological cycle and only specific scenes of the Old Testament which had a symbolic meaning were represented in the apse.[95] Thus the Genesis cycle of Aght'amar retains an early decorative system as well as elements of a cycle considered appropriate for a church. Old and New Testament scenes could face one another on the walls of a basilica, but the disposition had to be modified in a church built on a centralized plan. This has been done at Aght'amar, with due regard for the symbolic meaning of the church structure.

The central dome represents the heavens; the artist has depicted here the terrestrial paradise in which man was placed and which he lost through the Fall. The scenes from the life of Christ painted on the walls of the church recall that paradise lost will be regained through the Incarnation and Sacrifice of Christ. The parallelism between the Old and the New Testament, explained by Greek and Latin Church Fathers, is also propounded in Armenian writings. In a text ascribed to the eighth century which deals particularly with the symbolism of the Christian edifice, the church is said to be "a paradise planted by God which evil cannot enter; for from that first one we were expelled through the wiles of the serpent, but we enter this one through Christ . . . In that other paradise was planted the tree of life, forbidden to the first-born; while here we have the cross of life, planted by the same planter, and which has taken root and has blossomed through His life-giving blood."[96] This, and similar passages, fully explain the presence of the Genesis cycle and its relation to the Gospel scenes; as in the sculptures of the outer façades, and in an even clearer manner, the parallelism of the two Testaments is set forth by the paintings.

Although only a few scenes of the Creation remain and these are in a poor state of preservation, the comparison of typical details with other representations enables us to see that the Aght'amar cycle belongs to a recension which has not hitherto been known through any East Christian example. These typical details are: the Creator appearing in human form; the fully formed bust of Eve emerging from Adam's side; and Adam and Eve expelled by an angel. In one of the early recensions of Bible illustration known through the fifth-century Greek manuscript known as the "Cotton Bible" and through allied monuments, the Creator appears in human form, but He removes the rib from Adam's side and it is He, not an angel, who drives Adam and Eve out of the Garden of Eden.[97] In another recension, preserved in the later copies of the Greek Octateuchs, we see Eve's fully formed bust in the Creation scene, and the angel in the Expulsion, but the Creator does not appear in human form; His presence is merely suggested by means of the divine hand and rays descending from the segment of sky.[98]

The characteristic features of the Aght'amar cycle, in fact almost every detail of the different scenes, find their closest parallels in the twelfth-century Sicilian mosaics at the Cappella Palatina, in Palermo, and at the Cathedral of Monreale, as well as on the reliefs of a silver cross of approximately the same date, the so-called Cross of Constantine in the Lateran.[99] In the Sicilian mosaics the Expulsion scene follows the image of the cherubim guarding the gate, and Adam and Eve are clothed, but on the silver cross of the Lateran the Expulsion is represented first, and Adam and Eve are nude, as in the paintings of Aght'amar. Only the draped figure which seemed to form part of the scene of the Creation of Eve at Aght'amar does not have its counterpart in the monuments just mentioned. The painting is unfortunately badly damaged, but it is perhaps worth recalling that in the Carolingian Bibles, which are also derived from Early Christian models, an angel sometimes appears in the background of the Creation scenes.

The close correspondence between these Armenian paintings of the tenth century and the Western examples of the twelfth century can only be explained by their ultimate derivation from a common source. Thus the paintings of Aght'amar are important witnesses of an early cycle and, incidentally, they help to prove, what had already been surmised, that the Old Testament scenes in the Sicilian churches are based on an East Christian model.

The Christological cycle depicts the major events in the life of Christ beginning with the Annunciation, and a few episodes of lesser importance. The cycle probably extended to the Pentecost and included the Dormition of the Virgin, as mentioned above.

The infancy of Christ is illustrated in some detail, but it should be noted that the painters of Aght'amar have excluded the apocryphal episodes, such as the testing of Mary by the water of oath, or Elizabeth fleeing from the massacre with the infant John, which found great favor with the Cappadocian painters and other artists of the Christian East. The miracles have also been omitted with the exception of the Raising of Lazarus, which belongs to the cycle of the major events of Christ's life, and of the wedding feast at Cana. The place assigned to the wedding at Cana confers a particular meaning to it and sets it apart from other miracles. By its position in the same exedra as the Baptism and the Transfiguration, the first miracle through which Christ's divine power became manifest is grouped with the first two theophanies. The miracle at Cana was often interpreted as a figuration of the Epiphany;[100] the painter of Aght'amar has departed from the usual chronological sequence and by representing it after the Transfiguration, instead of before it, he has placed it as a pendant to the Baptism.

In the Passion cycle, scenes which frequently appear elsewhere have been omitted, for instance, the Descent from the cross and the Burial; while the Resurrection is represented both by the visit of the holy women to the sepulcher and the Harrowing of hell. The most interesting departure from current usage occurs in the substitution of the anointment of Christ at Bethany for the Last Supper. Again, as in the case of the wedding at Cana, the chronological sequence has been intentionally modified and the scene follows the Entry into Jerusalem instead of preceding it. The anointment scene has been grouped with the washing of the apostles' feet, thereby emphasizing the parallelism between the two events. This parallelism would easily occur to an Armenian painter, or to the person who devised the entire iconographic program. In the ceremony of the washing of the feet, regularly performed in Armenian churches, the bishop or priest anoints as well as washes the feet of the clerics who symbolize the apostles. Before doing this he pours the chrism crosswise into the vessel of water, and in the prayer which he recites he mentions the anointment of Christ's feet, adding that it is in memory of that event, and following that example that the oil is blessed, so that the grace of God may abide in those whose feet will be washed and anointed.[101]

The substitution of the anointment of Christ for the Last Supper, of which no other example is known in church decoration, is significant: it shows that the usual cycle of scenes was modified in order to stress a particular usage of the Armenian rite. The composition of Christ appearing to Mary Magdalene which, if my interpretation is correct, includes the image of King Gagik, shows an even more interesting departure from current practice, and as with the sculptures this modification is to be explained by the fact that Aght'amar is a palatine church.

If we exclude the kneeling figure of Mary Magdalene, the compositional scheme repeats that of the ruler standing in adoration, or prayer, before Christ, a type which, like the image of the ruler offering in homage to Christ the church he had erected, belongs to the imperial iconography of Byzantium. These types developed in the Byzantine Empire after the triumph of Orthodoxy in 843, but whereas in all the examples that have been preserved the emperor stands alone before Christ or the Virgin, here the portrait of Gagik has been added to a Gospel scene. The introduction of a living person into the Gospel narrative is alien to the Byzantine spirit. A mosaic of the Church of the Holy Apostles, in Constantinople, destroyed after the Turkish conquest, might, at first, seem to contradict what has just been stated. In describing the composition of the holy women at the sepulcher, Nikolaos Mesarites, an author of the twelfth century, writes that it included the portrait of "the man who depicted these things with his hand, as he is to be seen, standing upright at the tomb of the Lord, like some sleepless watcher."[102] But these words suggest that one of the soldiers guarding the sepulcher was represented with the features and costume of the mosaicist himself, rather than that an extraneous person was added to the scene, as he is at Aght'amar.

Armenian religious art was bound by less rigid rules than Byzantine iconography, and in works of later dates we find other examples of portraits of donors in Gospel scenes. In a Gospel of the fourteenth century Queen Mariun, who commissioned the manuscript, kneels in adoration next to the cross in the scene of the Descent from the cross, and her name is inscribed in large letters above her head.[103] The queen is also included, though in a less prominent position, in the scenes of the Nativity and the Entry into Jerusalem. The composition of Christ appearing to Mary Magdalene is painted at Aght'amar directly opposite the gallery where Gagik prayed, far from all others so that he might converse with God undisturbed. Gagik's image appeared then in the paintings, praying before Christ, just as he stood on the west façade, offering to Him the model of the church he had erected.

Before we pass to the study of the individual scenes, a few more words should be said about the choice of subjects. The portraits painted in the diagonal niches and on the piers represent, without exception, holy bishops none of whom can be identified, for the inscriptions are now illegible. The usual practice was to depict prophets, patriarchs, and various categories in the hierarchy of saints, such as warrior saints, martyrs, monks, hermits, and so forth. Some of these had been represented on the façades of the church and the painters may not have wished to repeat them, but whatever the reason may have been, the exclusive use of bishop portraits is most unusual.

The iconographic study of the different scenes shows on the one hand the persistence of Early Christian types, and, on the other, variants which are characteristic of Armenian art. I shall limit my remarks to some of the more important examples.

The central part of the Nativity, with Mary and Joseph seated on either side of the manger, follows the compositional scheme of the Early Christian period, familiar through the reliefs on the ampullae, that is the phials containing oil from the holy sites of Palestine, or other well-known examples such as the beautiful silk textile in the Sancta Sanctorum, in Rome.[104] But through the addition of the adoration of the shepherds and the magi, the composition conforms to the complex type favored by Armenian artists. It is also a characteristic of Armenian paintings to include Peter and John in the scene of the holy women at the sepulcher, but once again the central part of the composition, namely the sepulcher itself, recalls the representations on the Palestinian ampullae or on kindred works like the reliquary cover in the Sancta Sanctorum, in Rome.[105] As in these objects brought from the Holy Land, there is a definite attempt to represent the actual monument erected over Christ's tomb, with its conical roof and the lattice-work grilles between the columns. The stone covered with a cloth is the "rolled stone" of Christ's sepulcher which was used as an altar, in Jerusalem, on special occasions. But the general aspect of the building has been modified through the addition of acanthus leaves around the roof, and in this respect it finds its closest parallels in the "tempietto," or image of the sepulcher, painted in several Armenian Gospel manuscripts of the tenth century.[106]

In the Crucifixion, the *colobium* worn by Christ, the inclusion of the lance and sponge bearers as well as of the two robbers, the way in which the robbers are represented with their arms tied behind the cross, are once again characteristic of the primitive iconography of this scene. But it should be noted that Christ is represented dead, with eyes closed, a type which, according to recent investigations, was already in use in the ninth century.[107] One detail differentiates this composition from other known examples; the lance bearer is an elderly man wearing a helmet and a chlamys instead of the usual youthful figure clad in a short tunic. In the apocryphal Acts of Pilate the soldier who pierced Christ's side is called Longinus, and this name is often inscribed next to him, beginning with the earliest representations. But in the apocryphal life of Longinus, the name is identified with the centurion who was present at the Crucifixion and who bore witness, saying, "Truly, this was the son of God." It is this confusion between the lance bearer and the centurion which has led the painter of Aght'amar to represent him in military costume.

The wedding feast at Cana, one of the favorite subjects of the Early Christian period, still figures in the narrative cycle of the older group of Cappadocian chapels, but it is left out of the restricted number of scenes selected for the decoration of the churches of the Middle Byzantine period. The place assigned to it at Aght'amar stressed, as noted above, the theological meaning of this event; the iconography of the scene, on the contrary, gives to it an almost secular character. During the early centuries only the miracle was usually represented: Christ touches the jars with His wand; sometimes the steward pouring the water is also represented. Later the artists of the Christian East added the banquet scene, but they still showed Christ turning the water into wine. At Aght'amar the miracle is suggested but not actually portrayed, for while the servant pours the water into a crater under the supervision of the master of the feast, Christ remains seated at the table. The banquet itself is the dominant feature of the composition; we see not only the guests gathered around the table and the servants who wait on them, but also, in the foreground, two young men dressed in contemporary costume, seated cross-legged and holding wine glasses, exactly like the king represented in the middle of the vine frieze on the east façade. This characteristic group of young men drinking reappears in Armenian manuscripts of a later date and almost exclusively in those which have been illustrated in the general area of Lake Van.[108] No signs of repainting are apparent on the photographs of this scene at Aght'amar, and we have no reason to suppose that the young men were added later to the composition for the space next to the window would, in that case, have originally been empty. We must therefore conclude that the iconographic variant of Aght'amar persisted, and that we should probably have found intermediary examples between this tenth-century painting and the fourteenth-century manuscripts of this region, if they had not all been destroyed.

The simple composition of the Harrowing of hell or descent of Christ into limbo includes two angels. The apocryphal Gospel of Nicodemus, on which this Byzantine type of the Resurrection is based, mentions the angels who accompanied Christ and to whom He delivered Satan. The artists of the Middle Byzantine period occasionally represent angels flying in the sky; later, during the Palaeologan period, the angels are sometimes shown binding the hands and feet of the demons; but in no other example do we see them walking behind Christ, as they do at Aght'amar. The closest parallel that may be cited is a fragmentary mosaic from the ninth-century decoration of the Chapel of San Zeno, at the Church of Santa Prassede, in Rome, where an angel's head appears to the right of Christ.[109]

Other iconographic variants may be due to spatial requirements. The crowding of the Raising of Lazarus and the Entry into Jerusalem into the left half of the west exedra probably forced the painter to eliminate from the first scene the group of Jews who were present at the miracle and the attendants unwinding Lazarus' shroud or removing the door of the tomb; and probably for the same reason he placed behind the tomb the two sisters who, in all other examples, kneel at Christ's feet. Elsewhere, having a larger area at his disposal, the painter elaborated the composition; in the scene of the massacre of the innocents he depicted on the pier, to the right of the west exedra, the group of mourning women, just as the sculptor had represented, on the south façade, the people of Nineveh in the story of Jonah. The restraint with which the bereaved mothers express their grief contrasts with the violent gestures that one sees in the Cappadocian frescoes or in Coptic manuscripts, where the women wail and tear their hair.[110] This restraint is characteristic of all the paintings of Aght'amar and puts them on a different plane from the popular art of Cappadocia.

One last scene must be considered, namely the painting above the south door, immediately under the king's gallery, which unfortunately is so badly preserved. The composition, with the bust of Christ in the upper part of the conch and two rows of standing figures below, has marked affinities with the miniatures of two Byzantine manuscripts of the ninth century. One of these is to be seen in the copy of the Christian Topography of Cosmas Indicopleustes in the Vatican Library, and it illustrates a passage in which this writer of the sixth century explains the structure of the universe. In this example the figures are enclosed in a rectangular frame, rounded at the top. In the uppermost part Christ, blessing, is seated on a throne. In the three zones below Him we see, first, the angels who inhabit the space between the uppermost heaven and earth, then the men who dwell on earth, and finally the busts of the dead who are returning to life.[111] This same scheme has been used in another ninth-century manuscript, the Sacra Parallela of John of Damascus at the Bibliothèque Nationale (Paris Gr. 923), for a representation of the Second Coming of Christ. Christ is again enthroned in the uppermost part of the rectangle, which is also rounded; below appear two adoring angels, then a group of men inside a jeweled enclosure which represents Jerusalem on high. In a separate image, further down, we see the damned in the jaws of hell. As A. Grabar has shown, both these compositions represent the Second Coming of Christ, for though the miniature in the Cosmas manuscript exactly corresponds to his description of the universe, the painter has inscribed above it the words addressed by Jesus to the righteous who will inherit the Kingdom of God: "Come, ye blessed of my Father" (Matthew 25.34).[112]

It has already been suggested that these two miniatures were probably derived from a monumental composition of the Second Coming which preceded the fully developed type of the Last Judgment as we see it in Byzantine art from the eleventh century on. Aght'amar now brings us the proof, for, in spite of minor differences, we have the same general scheme as in the two ninth-century miniatures: Christ in the uppermost part and, below, two rows of nimbed figures, the righteous who have inherited the Kingdom of God. It is possible that the painting originally extended below the second zone of figures and that the resurrection of the dead was represented in this part.[113]

Like the composition of the wedding feast at Cana, that of the Second Coming of Christ reappears in manuscripts illustrated in the region of Lake Van. In these miniatures the iconography of the Last Judgment differs from the fully developed Byzantine type adopted by Armenian painters working in other centers. We see, in the upper part, Christ enthroned on the tetramorphic throne and the Virgin and John the Baptist at His sides; below are one or two rows of figures standing in front view; the lowest zone shows the weighing of the souls.[114] If we eliminate the figures which belong to the Last Judgment itself, namely, the Virgin and John the Baptist interceding to Christ, and the weighing of the souls, we have the principal elements of the Aght'amar composition: the group of the elect standing below the image of Christ.

The Last Judgment is usually depicted on the west wall of the churches but the architectural plan of Aght'amar and the distribution of the Gospel scenes arranged in chronological order did not leave enough free space in the west exedra. However, as it was placed above the south door, the cycle begins in the south exedra, above the royal gallery, with the Annunciation, and also ends there, below this gallery, with the vision of Christ's Second Coming and the resurrection of the dead.

As mentioned previously, the paintings have marked affinities with the sculptures and are the products of the same workshop; we have the same hieratic style, the same motionless figures. Since the subjects that have been represented inside the church required a larger number of figures, and since space was restricted because many scenes had to be depicted, the compositions are crowded, one passes from one scene to the next without any break, without even a line of demarcation. The painters do not strive to achieve a plastic, three-dimensional form, nor do they try to stir the emotions of the beholders by an exaggerated portrayal of sorrow. They are interested in the linear schemes of the draperies and in a simplification which tends toward abstraction. There is undoubtedly a certain degree of awkwardness in the rendering of these stocky forms, yet their severe dignity and their monumental quality makes them strangely impressive. Christ and many of the other figures gazing into space hardly seem to be participating in any action. They are absorbed in their thoughts and exist in a world far removed from ours. The elimination of all episodic detail (with the exception of the miracle at Cana) accentuates this feeling of unreality despite the denseness of the compositions.

This abstract style is in marked contrast with that of a contemporary work of art which also belongs to this region. One of the few illustrated Armenian manuscripts of this period and, incidentally, one of the finest, is a Gospel offered by Queen Mlk'e, the wife of Gagik, to the Monastery of Varag.[115] The portraits of the Evangelists and the large full-page miniature of the Ascension are painted in a bold impressionistic style. The three-dimensional figures with their varied poses, their freedom of movement, and the emphasis on color modeling rather than on linear patterns belong to an artistic trend totally different from the one represented at Aght'amar. The model of Queen Mlk'e's Gospel must have been a work of a much earlier period, of Alexandrian origin, for a crocodile hunt has been represented in two of the lunettes, and octopuses and other fish fill another lunette. The scarcity of surviving monuments makes it impossible for us to decide whether Queen Mlk'e's manuscript is an isolated example or whether it shows that the traditions of late Classical art, which we know had penetrated into Armenia in the early centuries of our era, had persisted in some works until the tenth century. This much can be said: the paintings of Aght'amar are more in keeping with the style of the majority of surviving monuments and, therefore, more representative of Armenian art. The earlier stages of this style can be seen in some of the reliefs and paintings of the sixth and seventh centuries; the miniatures of the Etchmiadzin Gospel, illustrated in 989, represent a later stage of the same artistic trend.[116]

The paintings of Aght'amar throw new light on many aspects of East Christian art. The Genesis cycle depicted in the drum of the dome shows a type of church decoration hitherto unknown in early Medieval art; the iconography of these scenes has revealed a recension which, likewise, was not known through any East Christian example but only in the mosaics of the Sicilian churches in the twelfth century. As in the sculptures of the façades, we see in some of the representations the persistence of Early Christian types; other details, like the dead Christ on the cross, indicate that the painters of Aght'amar were aware of the new developments in the art of Constantinople. Old and new forms are combined but not followed blindly; modifications are introduced in conformity with the Armenian ritual; and a bold innovation is made by including the founder's portrait in a Gospel scene. Once again, as in the sculptures but in a different manner, the palatine character of this church becomes manifest.

Although built in a remote area, the Church of the Holy Cross of Aght'amar is not a provincial monument but a major work of Medieval art, a unique example for this period with its rich and original sculptures and its interesting cycle of paintings. It has withstood many vicissitudes for more than a thousand years and is still in a surprisingly good state of preservation. But, now abandoned, with doors and windows broken, it has begun to show signs of rapid deterioration. The parapet of the royal tribune, with its row of animals in high relief, has completely disappeared; comparison with photographs taken before 1914 shows a number of fresh breaks in the reliefs and carvings in the round which adorn the façades; shrubs are growing in the cracks of the stones and will soon dislodge them; the rain blowing in through the broken windows and seeping through the damaged roof will further damage the paintings which were already flaking off. It is to be hoped that before it is too late careful measures will be taken to preserve this rare example of Medieval art.

TOMBSTONES AND CROSS STONES

THERE is an old cemetery behind the church, extending from the southeast corner to the north side. The catholicoses and members of the monastic community were buried here, some of their tombstones or the cross stones they erected in their lifetime still survive and they are interesting records of the later history of Aght'amar.

Among the examples reproduced here, the oldest dated cross stone is that of the Catholicos Stephen IV (Step'anos) who ruled from *ca*. 1336 to 1346 (figs. 71, 72). He was the grandson of Sefedin Ark'ayun, a wealthy member of the Artzruni family who at one time owned the entire island, and two of whose sons and another grandson ascended the patriarchal throne of Aght'amar. The cross stone erected by Stephen is now mutilated, and large sections of the carvings have been mercilessly hacked. The inscription carved at the bottom begins: "In the year 789 [which corresponds to A.D. 1340], I, Ter Step'anos, vicar of Aght'amar, an Artzruni by birth, I erected this cross as an intercessor before God for myself, and for my mother T'aguhi, and for my sister Nuri Khat'un, and for my sister's daughter Khuand." The remaining lines are not visible on the photograph.[117]

By comparing the fragmentary remains with other Armenian cross stones of this period we can reconstruct the general design of the decoration.[118] In the central field, limited by an arch inscribed in a rectangle, a large cross, framed by half palmettes, was carved. Below are four small crosses under arches which are also inscribed in rectangles. The arms of the large cross, the arches, and the rectangular bands around the small crosses are decorated with a twisted-rope motif or guilloche; floral interlaces fill the triangular spaces between the large arch and the rectangle. Bands of linear interlace surround this rectangle on three sides. The wide upper interlace is formed by continuous strands which, by interweaving, delineate three large ten-point stars and another which is incomplete; a rosette marks the center of each star. There must have been originally another row of ten-point stars and a narrow plaited border surrounded this part of the decoration. A different type of linear ornament appears on the narrower side bands: it consists of separate geometric forms instead of continuous strands. The octagons are here connected with one another by means of interweaving hexagons: complete hexagons in the vertical axis and half hexagons in the transverse axis. The intersecting strands of these hexagons determine eight-point stars in the middle of each octagon, and rosettes again mark the center of each star.

Linear ornaments and, in particular, different types of interlace appear at an early date in Armenia; and a continuous line of development can be followed through the centuries. The monuments of the tenth and succeeding centuries present a vast repertoire of the most intricate designs; wide bands of interlace frame the doors and windows of the churches and they are the favorite motifs chosen for the decoration of cross stones.[119]

The second dated stele at Aght'amar belongs to the fifteenth century (fig. 73); it was still intact when Bachmann photographed it in 1911 but it too has now been broken and again some of the carving has been hacked off.[120] The inscription reads: "In the year 893[A.D.1444] I, Ter Zak'aria, Catholicos of the Armenians by the power of God and with His assistance, I erected this cross as an intercessor before God for my soul. You who bow down before it, remember [me] in Jesus Christ. Remember in Christ, Grigor, the sculptor."

Zak'aria was also an Artzruni; in the memorial notice of a contemporary manuscript he is referred to as a man of royal descent, from the family of King Gagik. He ruled from 1434 to 1464 and he is one of the most prominent among the catholicoses of Aght'amar, even occupying for several years the patriarchal throne of Etchmiadzin.[121] The scriptorium of Aght'amar was very active at this time and a number of manuscripts, some with rich illuminations, have survived.

The photograph published by Bachmann enables us to see the entire decoration of the stele of which only a fragment remains. The cross, raised on a triangular plaited base, is framed by palmette scrolls and interlacing strands wound around the arms of the cross. The large palmettes, with curving tips, are of a type which appears on dated steles of the thirteenth century, and on these the scrolls fill the entire background, as they do here. Bands of linear interlace frame the central section on all four sides. The upper band, wider than the other three, is decorated with the same design as the preceding stele, that is, continuous strands which, by interlacing, determine ten-point stars marked with a rosette at the center. The ornament of the other three bands appears, at first sight, to reproduce the design of the side bands of the preceding example, but it is actually a variation of this motif. The principal elements are circles, not octagons, and the hexagons and half-hexagons, instead of being separate forms which intersect one another, are determined by the interlaces of two continuous strands. Rosettes again decorate the central space of each circle, which has the shape of an eight-point star.

Through the accuracy of the carving and the elegance and variety of the designs, these cross stones, now sadly mutilated, are excellent examples of the decorative sculpture of the fourteenth and fifteenth centuries. The background has been deeply hollowed out and the design stands out clearly against the shadows of the background. The workmanship of some of the other tombstones which are still intact is somewhat inferior in quality, the carving is more shallow, and the different motifs are not as sharply defined. The general composition is, however, the same: a large cross in the center and ornamental bands around it. On the stele reproduced in figure 74, the cross placed under an arch is raised on a plaited base and framed by a palmette scroll like the stele of the Catholicos Zak'aria; the arms of the cross are decorated with a guilloche as in the first example. The ornament of the wide upper band is basically the same as that of the side borders on Zak'aria's stele: circles, placed here in two rows, are connected by hexagons formed by continuous strands. But the design no longer has the clarity and accuracy of the preceding example and it would be difficult to recognize the component elements if we did not have the earlier stele. At the sides interlacing units alternate with large trefoils and are crowned by a cross. On another stele, the central section is set back from the frame. The large cross is again surrounded by a palmette scroll, and there are three small crosses under it. A half palmette scroll runs along the side bands, and on the entablature interweaving strands frame three-lobed leaves.

Several of the cross stones are much simpler. The shape of the cross is usually hollowed out and the surrounding floral and geometric designs are incised (fig. 77). Two catholicoses of the nineteenth century erected more elaborate monuments. The tombstone of Khatchatur Mokatsi is arched instead of being rectangular (fig. 75); the inscription which occupies the greater part of the central section reads as follows: "This cross [is an] intercessor to the Only begotten for the salvation of the pontiff, His Grace Khatchatur, who departed to the Lord in heaven in the year of the Armenians 1300 [A.D. 1851], on the twelfth of June. January 26." The last date must be that of the erection of the stele. Above this inscription is an interlace cross on a triangular base, flanked by two ornate lozenges; further up a dove is flying down, and at its sides are two shell-like ornaments. Slightly set in under the inscription we see the bust figure of the Catholicos, wearing his miter; to the right is a large crescent and to the left a small, flying angel and the large disc of the sun. The outer frame is decorated with a trefoil scroll, terminated at either end of the uprights by small rosettes; an angel head, with large wings, is carved inside the stepped base of the slender column. An architrave, interrupted at the middle, separates the rectangular section from the tympanum; it is decorated with triangular pendants which imitate the stalactite motif. Similar triangular motifs project inward from the arch and from the slender columns of the uprights.

On the last example, which is partly broken, the portrait of the Catholicos occupies the entire surface (fig. 76). He wears the patriarchal cope decorated with floral motifs; he is crowned with the miter and holds the crosier. Two seraphim are carved in low reliefs, one close to his right shoulder, the other next to his head. This must be the headstone of the elaborate tomb of the Catholicos Khatchatur Shiroyian, described by Lynch, which was dedicated on September 12, 1893. Khatchatur died two years later, on December 22, 1895. According to Lynch, figures of apostles were represented on the sides of the recumbent portion of the tomb, and these reliefs were "coloured in gaudy reds and greens and blues. Upon the upper surface of the slab was engraved a long inscription, and beneath the inscription the grand emblem of the double-headed eagle, with cross and mitre, the eagle of Vaspurakan."[122]

NOTES

NOTES

1. H. F. B. Lynch, *Armenia. Travels and Studies* (London, 1901), II, 38–39.

2. *Ibid.*, p. 129.

3. Thomas Artzruni, *History of the House of the Artzrunis* (Tiflis, 1917, in Armenian), pp. 466–467. French translation in M. Brosset, *Collection d'historiens arméniens* (St. Petersburg, 1874), I, 229–230. Translations in this volume are my own, as are all other translations of quotations from Armenian. Thomas Artzruni dates the coronation of Gagik after the imprisonment and death of the Bagratid King Smbat in 914, but the account of John Catholicos seems more reliable and Gagik was probably crowned in 908. Cf. Brosset, p. 229, note.

4. Artzruni, p. 406; Brosset, p. 205.

5. Artzruni, pp. 405–406; Brosset, pp. 204–205.

6. Artzruni, pp. 475–477; Brosset, pp. 234–235.

7. Artzruni, pp. 478–483; Brosset, pp. 236–239.

8. Artzruni, pp. 481–482; Brosset, p. 238.

9. Artzruni, pp. 485–487; Brosset, pp. 239–241. Neither the architect Manuel nor the cleric who was entrusted with the sculptural decoration is mentioned in the preceding pages.

10. E. Lalayan, "The Famous Monasteries of Vaspurakan. The Monastery of the Holy Cross at Aght'amar" (in Armenian), *Azgagrakan Handes*, 12 (1910): 208.

11. N. Akinian, *History of the Catholicoses of Aght'amar* (Vienna, 1920, in Armenian), pp. 8–11.

12. Lalayan, "Monastery of the Holy Cross," p. 209; Akinian, *The Catholicoses of Aght'amar*, p. 44.

13. Artzruni, *The House of the Artzrunis*, pp. 523–524.

14. Austen H. Layard, *Discoveries in the Ruins of Nineveh and Babylon with Travels in Armenia, Kurdistan and the Desert Being the Result of a Second Expedition Undertaken for the Trustees of the British Museum* (London, 1853), pp. 413–414.

15. Lynch, *Armenia*, II, 129–135.

16. Walter Bachmann, *Kirchen und Moscheen in Armenien und Kurdistan* (Leipzig, 1913), pp. 40–47, pl. 31–40.

17. Joseph Strzygowski, *Die Baukunst der Armenier und Europa* (Vienna, 1918), see especially pp. 82–84, 289–296.

18. See especially Ep'rikian in *Pasmaveb*, 1897; Akinian, *The Catholicoses of Aght'amar*; H. Oskian, *The Monasteries of Vaspurakan Van* (Vienna, 1940, in Armenian), I, 86–133.

19. Lalayan, "Monastery of the Holy Cross," pp. 197–212.

20. A. Sakisian, "Notes on the Sculpture of the Church of Akhthamar," *The Art Bulletin*, 25 (1943): 346–357; E. Coche de la Ferté, "Une Eglise inaccessible," *L'Oeil*, Oct. 1956, pp. 4–9; R. Burton, J. Donat and P. Koralek, "Achthamar," *The Architectural Review*, vol. 123, no. 734 (1958), pp. 174–181; and S. Der Nersessian, *Armenia and the Byzantine Empire* (Cambridge, Mass., 1945), pp. 90–96.

21. G. Goyan, *2000 let Armianskago teatro* (Moscow, 1952), II, 181–323. Since 1959 the following studies have been published: travel notes by Merry Ottin and Jérome Camilly in *Connaissance des arts*, Nov. 1960, pp. 54–59; a long article, primarily on the vine scroll, by Katharina Otto-Dorn, "Türkisch Islamisches Bildgut in den Figurenreliefs von Achthamar," *Anatolia*, 6 (1961): 99–167; and a book by M. Ş. Ipşiroğlu, *Die Kirche von Achthamar. Bauplastik im Leben des Lichtes* (Berlin and Mainz, 1963).

22. Bachmann, *Kirchen und Moscheen*, pl. 32; Lalayan, "Monastery of the Holy Cross," p. 200.

23. L. Khatchikian, *Colophons of Armenian Manuscripts of the Fifteenth Century. Second Part* (Erevan, 1958, in Armenian), p. 308. See also Ep'rikian in *Pazmaveb*, 1897, p. 208. A notice in a manuscript of later date records a second reconstruction of the dome in 1556: Lalayan, "Monastery of the Holy Cross," p. 198.

24. Akinian, *The Catholicoses of Aght'amar*, pp. 157–158, corrects the date of 1803 given by Lalayan.

25. Strzygowski, *Baukunst*, pp. 76–78, 89–94.

26. Der Nersessian, *Armenia and the Byzantine Empire*, pp. 88–90, pl. X.1; Strzygowski, *Baukunst*, pp. 427–430.

27. The cross stone embedded in the side wall of the belfry is older than this construction.

28. Lalayan, "Monastery of the Holy Cross," p. 200.

29. If the animal is not a purely decorative element, it may have been included to suggest that David had just left his father's flocks to come and fight against Goliath.

30. *Soobshcheniia gosudarstvennogo Ermitazha* (Leningrad, 1945), p. 23; G. Hovsep'ian, *Khaghpakians or Proshians* (Vagharshapat, 1928, in Armenian), figs. 96–97.

31. Strzygowski, *Baukunst*, p. 284, fig. 318.

32. R. H. Charles, *The Acrocrypha and Pseudepigrapha of the Old Testament* (Oxford, 1913), p. 663.

33. For a comparison of the sculptures of Aght'amar with the image of paradise see A. Grabar, "La 'Sedia di San Marco' à Venise," *Cahiers archéologiques*, 7 (1954): 29–30.

34. Artzruni, *The House of the Artzrunis*, p. 88; Brosset, *Collection d'historiens arméniens*, p. 40.

35. P. Peeters, "La légende de saint Jacques de Nisibe," *Analecta Bollandiana*, 38 (1920): 336–337, 342–373.

36. *Lives and Martyrdoms of Saints* (Venice, 1813, in Armenian), V, 272.

37. Der Nersessian, *Armenia and the Byzantine Empire*, p. 88, pl. X.1. For other examples of portraits in medallions see A. Grabar, "L'Imago clipeata chrétienne," *Comptes-rendus de l'Académie des Inscriptions et Belles Lettres* (1957), pp. 209–213.

38. Der Nersessian, pp. 87–88, pl. IX; J. Baltrusaitis, *Etudes sur l'art médiéval en Géorgie et en Arménie* (Paris, 1929), pl. LXX; B. Arak'elian, *Armenian Figured Sculpture of the IV–VII Centuries* (Erevan, 1949, in Armenian), figs. 9–10, 19–21.

39. G. I. Tchubinashvili, *Pamiatniki tipa Dzhvari* (Tiflis, 1948), pl. 60.

40. C. O. Nordstrom, "Some Jewish Legends in Byzantine Art," *Byzantion*, 25–27 (1955–1957): 505–508.

41. For instance in Paris gr. 139 and Paris gr. 510: H. Omont, *Miniatures des plus anciens manuscrits grecs de la Bibliothèque nationale* (Paris, 1929), pls. XII and XX.

42. K. Weitzmann, "Die Illustration der Septuaginta," *Münchner Jahrbuch der bildenden Kunst*. 3–4 (1952–1953): 119.

43. *British Museum. Catalogue of the Greek Coins of Lycia, Pamphylia and Pisidia*, by George F. Hill (London, 1897), pl. XXXVI, nos. 3–5.

44. P. Perdrizet, *Negotium perambulans in tenebris* (Strasbourg-Paris, 1922); A. Grabar, *L'Empereur dans l'art byzantin* (Paris, 1936), pp. 47–50.

45. K. Kafadarian, *Gorod Dvin i ego Raskopki* (Erevan, 1952, in Armenian with Russian title), p. 145, figs. 114–115.

46. Strzygowski, *Baukunst*, p. 290, fig. 329.

47. L. A. Durnovo, *Kratkaia istoriia drevnearmianskoi zhivopisi* (Erevan, 1957), p. 9; Strzygowski, pp. 498–499, fig. 530.

48. *Selected Lives of Saints* (Venice, 1874, in Armenian), II, 296–297.

49. H. Delehaye, *Les Légendes grecques des saints militaires* (Paris, 1904), pp. 115–117; *Lives and Martyrdoms of Saints* (in Armenian), II, 354–355, V, 189; K. Krumbacher, "Der heilige Georg in der griechischen Uberlieferung," *Abhandlungen der König. Bayer. Akad. der Wissenschaften, philos.-hist. Klasse,* 25.3 (1911). The cavalier saints appear frequently in Georgian art (Baltrusaitis, *L'Art médiéval en Géorgie et en Arménie,* pl. LXVII) and the crowned man trampled by Saint George is designated as Diocletian. See in particular G. N. Tschubinaschvili, *Georgian Repoussé Work VIII to XVIII centuries,* Academy of Sciences of the Georgian SSR, Institute of History of Georgian Art (Tiflis, 1957), pls. 92–98.

50. Joseph M. Upton, "The Expedition to Ctesiphon, 1931–32," *Bulletin of the Metropolitan Museum of Art* (New York), 27 (1932): 188–197; H. Schmidt, "Figürliche sasanidische Stuckdekorationen aus Ktesiphon," *Ars Islamica,* 4 (1937): 175–184.

51. R. Ghirshman, *Bichâpour II. Les mosaïques sassanides* (Paris, 1956), pls. V–VII.

52. D. Schlumberger, "Les Fouilles de Qasr el-Heir el-Gharbi," *Syria,* 20 (1939): 324–360; A. Musil, *Kusejr 'Amra* (Vienna, 1907); R. W. Hamilton, *Khirbat al Mafjar. An Arabian Mansion in the Jordan Valley,* with a contribution by Dr. Oleg Grabar (Oxford, 1959).

53. E. Herzfeld, *Die Ausgrabungen von Samarra, III. Die Malereien* (Berlin, 1927).

54. R. Ghirshman, "Scènes de banquet sur l'argenterie sassanide," *Artibus Asiae,* 16 (1953): 51–76.

55. J. M. C. Toynbee and J. B. Ward Perkins, "Peopled Scrolls. A Hellenistic Motif in Imperial Art," *Papers of the British School at Rome,* 18 (1950): 1–43.

56. Hamilton, *Khirbat al Mafjar,* p. 203, pl. XLIX.

57. Kafadarian, *Gorod Dvin,* p. 144, fig. 113.

58. V. A. Abramian, *Remesla v Armenii IV–XVIIIvv* (Erevan, 1956, in Armenian with Russian summary), p. 98, fig. 32.

59. Goyan, *Armianskago teatro,* pp. 284–308.

60. Arthur Upham Pope, *Survey of Persian Art,* vol. IV, pl. 131; R. Ghirshman, *Bichâpour,* pp. 117–141 and pls. XXV–XXVI; M. I. Rostovtzev, "Dura and the Problem of Parthian Art," *Yale Classical Studies,* 5 (1935): 183f.

61. D. Tsonchev, "The Gold Treasure of Panagurishte," *Archaeology,* VIII.4 (1955): 224, figs. 9–10.

62. Ghirshman, *Bichâpour,* pl. XXVI; Kafadarian, *Gorod Dvin,* pp. 223–224, figs. 207–208.

63. J. Clédat, "Le Monastère et la nécropole de Baouit," *Mémoires publiés par les membres de l'Institut français d'archéologie orientale du Caire,* 12 (1904): pl. XXXVII; 39 (1916): pls. XVI–XVII.

64. A. Grabar, *L'Iconoclasme byzantin. Dossier archéologique* (Paris, 1957), pp. 144–145 and *passim.*

65. A. Grabar, *L'Empereur,* pp. 71–74.

66. Ugo Monneret de Villard, *Le pitture musulmane al soffitto della Cappella Palatina in Palermo* (Rome, 1950).

67. Edmond Pauty, *Bois sculptés d'églises coptes* (Cairo, 1930), pp. 13–25, pls. I–XVI.

68. Hamilton, *Khirbat al Mafjar,* pp. 240–241, pl. XLII, and figs. 25–26.

69. Baltrusaitis, *L'Art médiéval en Géorgie et en Arménie,* pls. LXX, LXXXI; Strzygowski, *Baukunst,* pp. 717–719; Arak'elian, *Armenian Figured Sculpture,* fig. 21.

70. A. Grabar, *L'Empereur,* pp. 56, 109–110.

71. Der Nersessian, *Armenia and the Byzantine Empire,* pp. 88–89, 96–97. The donor offering a model of the church to Christ had already been represented in 826 at the Church of Opiza, in Georgia. Sh. Ia. Amiranashvili, *Istoriia gruzinskogo iskusstva* (Moscow, 1950), pl. 111.

72. Artzruni, *The House of the Artzrunis*, p. 493; Brosset, *Collection d'historiens arméniens*, p. 244.

73. Schlumberger, "Les Fouilles," p. 329, pl. XLVI.1; B. Schulz and J. Strzygowski, "Mschatta," *Jahrbuch der Königlichen preuss. Kunstsammlungen* (1904), p. 223, fig. 15; Smirnov, *Argenterie orientale* (St. Petersburg, 1909), pl. XXV, no 64.

74. E. V. Bergmann, "Eine abbasidische Bild-münze," *Numismatische Zeitschrift*, 1 (Vienna, 1869) : 445–456; H. Nützel, "Eine Porträt-medaille des Chalifes al-Muktadir billah," *Zeitschrift für Numismatik* (Berlin), 22 (1900) : 259.

75. M. Bahrami, "A Gold Medal in the Freer Gallery of Art," *Archaeologica Orientalia in Memoriam Ernst Herzfeld* (New York, 1952), p. 20, fig. 4a.

76. *Ibid.*, p. 17, fig. 2; G. Wiet, "L'Islam et l'art musulman" in René Huyghe, *L'Art et l'homme* (Paris, 1957), II, 137, fig. 375.

77. R. B. Serjeant, "Materials for a History of Islamic Textiles up to the Mongol Conquest," *Ars Islamica*, 9 (1942) : 75; see also "The Armenian Caspian Group," 10 (1943) : 90–100.

78. B. Arak'elian, *Goroda i Remesla Armenii v IX–XIIIvv* (Erevan, 1958, in Armenian with Russian title), pp. 273–274.

79. Pope, *Survey of Persian Art*, vol. IV, pl. 166; Ghirshman, "Scènes de banquet," pp. 69–70 and fig. 17; Smirnoff, *Argenterie orientale*, pl. XX, no. 46; Tchubinashvili, *Pamiatniki tipa Dzhvari*, pl. 22; Basil Gray, "A Seljuq Hoard from Persia," *The British Museum Quarterly*, 13 (1939) : 73.

80. Walter Hauser and Charles K. Wilkinson, "The Museum's Excavations at Nishapur," *Bulletin of the Metropolitan Museum of Art* (New York), 37 (1942) : 118, fig. 45; Herzfeld, *Die Malereien*, pls. LXV, LXIX, and fig. 65.

81. A. Von Le Coq, *Bilderatlas zur Kunst und Kulturgeschichte Mittel-Asiens* (Berlin, 1925), figs. 6–9, 11, 15–36; D. Schlumberger, "Le Palais ghaznévide de Lashkari Bazar," *Syria*, 29 (1952) : 262–267, pls. XXXI–XXXII.

82. A. Grabar, "Le Succès des arts orientaux à la cour byzantine sous les Macédoniens," *Münchner Jahrbuch der bild. Kunst*, 2 (1951) : 34, fig. 2. For the spread of Sasanian and Islamic motifs see also A. Grabar, "Eléments sassanides et islamiques dans les enluminures des manuscrits espagnols du haut Moyen Age," *Arte del Primo Millennio. Atti del II° Convegno per lo Studio dell'Arte dell'Alto Medio Evo tenuto presso l'Università di Pavia nel Settembre 1950*, pp. 312–319.

83. Arak'elian, *Goroda i Remesla*, pl. XVII and pp. 276–277.

84. *Ibid.*, pl. LXVI; A. N. Svirin, *Miniatiura drevnei Armenii* (Moscow-Leningrad, 1939), p. 17.

85. K. A. C. Creswell, *Early Muslim Architecture* (Oxford, 1932), pls. 3c, 27a; Hamilton, *Khirbat al Mafjar*, pl. LXVIII.

86. V. M. Arutiunian, *Pamiatniki armianskogo zodchestva* (Moscow, 1951), fig. 44.

87. Ghirshman, *Bichâpour*, fig. 66 and pl. XXII.2; H. Seyrig, "Antiquités syriennes. Ornamenta Palmyrena antiquiora," *Syria*, 21 (1940) : pl. XXIX.

88. Lalayan, "Monastery of the Holy Cross," plate before p. 197; Bachmann, *Kirchen und Moscheen*, pl. 32; Strzygowski, *Baukunst*, pp. 298–299, fig. 337.

89. Der Nersessian, *Armenia and the Byzantine Empire*, pp. 110–112, and "Une Apologie des images du septième siècle," *Byzantion*, 17 (1944–1945), pp. 58–87.

90. Durnovo, *Drevnearmianskoi zhivopisi*, pp. 9 and 15, frontispiece, and pl. 1; Strzygowski, *Baukunst*, pp. 498, 705.

91. Strzygowski, *Baukunst*, fig. 337; Der Nersessian, *Armenia and the Byzantine Empire*, pl. XVII.1.

92. L. Wratislaw-Mitrovic and N. Okunev, "La Dormition de la Sainte Vierge dans la peinture médiévale orthodoxe," *Byzantinoslavica*, 3 (1931): 134–174.

93. H. Stern, "Les Mosaïques de l'église de Sainte-Constance à Rome," *Dumbarton Oaks Papers*, 12 (1958): 185–191; Fr. Camprubi Alemany, *El monumento paleocristiano de Cencelles (Tarragona)* (Barcelona, 1953); A. Fakhry, *The Egyptian Deserts. The Necropolis of El-Bagawat in Kharga Oasis* (Cairo, 1951), frontispiece and pls. XX–XXIV.

94. A. Grabar, "La Décoration des coupoles à Karye Camii et les peintures italiennes du Dugento," *Jahrbuch der österreichischen byzantinischen Gesellschaft*, 6 (1957): 111–124.

95. Remnants of a more extensive cycle may be seen in the Church of Peruštica, in Bulgaria, which belongs to the pre-Iconoclastic period. Episodes from the life of Moses and Daniel in the den of lions appear on the arches of the north exedra. A. Grabar, *La Peinture religieuse en Bulgarie* (Paris, 1928), pp. 23–25 and pl. II; A. Frolow, "L'Eglise rouge de Peruštica," *The Bulletin of the Byzantine Institute*, I (Paris, 1946): 37 and pls. XIV.2, XV.1, XVI.1.

96. Johannes Bapt. Aucher, *Domini Johannis Ozniensis Philosophi Armenorum Catholici Opera* (Venice, 1834), pp. 290–292.

97. J. J. Tikkanen, "Die Genesismosaiken von S. Marco in Venedig und ihr Verhältniss zu den Miniaturen der Cottonbibel," *Acta Societatis Scientiarum Fennicae*, 17 (1889); Rosalie B. Green, "The Adam and Eve Cycle in the Hortus Deliciarum," *Late Classical and Mediaeval Studies in Honour of Albert Mathias Friend, Jr.* (Princeton, 1955), pp. 340–347.

98. Th. Ouspensky, *L'Octateuque de la bibliothèque du Sérail à Constantinople* (Sofia, 1907), figs. 19–23; D. C. Hesseling, *Miniatures de l'Octateuque grec de Smyrne* (Leyden, 1909), figs. 9–10, 21, 23.

99. Otto Demus, *The Mosaics of Norman Sicily* (London, 1949), pls. 28–29. At Monreale the Creator is seated on the globe in some of the scenes; *ibid.*, pls. 95–97. C. Cecchelli, "Il Tesoro del Laterano. II. Oreficerie, Argenti, Smalti," *Dedalo*, 7 (1936–37): vol. 1, p. 246.

100. A. Grabar, *Martyrium* (Paris, 1946), II, 135–136.

101. *Avag Shabat'* (New Julfa, 1895, in Armenian), pp. 396–397. The antiphons sung in the medieval Western church during the ceremony of the washing of the feet include, almost always, references to Mary Magdalene anointing Christ's feet; cf. Ernst H. Kantorowicz, "The Baptism of the Apostles," *Dumbarton Oaks Papers*, 9–10 (1955–1956): 243–248.

102. Glanville Downey, "Nikolaos Mesarites: Description of the Church of the Holy Apostles at Constantinople," *Transactions of the American Philosophical Society*, 47 (1957): 884.

103. Der Nersessian, *Armenia and the Byzantine Empire*, pl. XXVII.2.

104. A. Grabar, *Les Ampoules de Terre Sainte* (Paris, 1958), pls. VII, LII. Philippe Lauer, "Le Trésor du Sancta Sanctorum," *Monuments Piot*, 15 (1906): pl. XVIII.5; see also pl. XIV.2 for the reliquary cover.

105. Grabar, *Les Ampoules de Terre Sainte*, pls. IX, XI, XXVI, XXVIII; Lauer, "Sancta Sanctorum," pl. XIV.2.

106. Paul A. Underwood, "The Fountain of Life in Manuscripts of the Gospels," *Dumbarton Oaks Papers*, 5 (1950): 89–95, figs. 34–38.

107. John R. Martin, "The Dead Christ on the Cross in Byzantine Art," *Late Classical and Mediaeval Studies in Honour of A. M. Friend, Jr.* (Princeton, 1955), pp. 189–196; A. Grabar, *L'Iconoclasme byzantin*, pp. 228–231.

108. S. Der Nersessian, *The Chester Beatty Library, A Catalogue of the Armenian Manuscripts* (Dublin, 1958), pp. xxxv–xxxvi, pl. 33b.

109. J. Wilpert, *Die römischen Mosaiken und Malereien der kirchlichen Bauten vom IV. bis XIII. Jahrhundert* (Freiburg in Brisgau, 1917), III, pl. 114.4.

110. G. de Jerphanion, *Les Eglises rupestres de Cappadoce* (Paris, 1925), pls. 37.4, 66.2; G. Millet, *Recherches sur l'iconographie de l'Evangile* (Paris, 1916), fig. 118.

111. C. Stornajolo, *Le miniature della topographia cristiana di Cosma Indicopleuste* (Milan, 1908), pl. 49.

112. Grabar, *L'Empereur*, pp. 251f, pl. XXXVIII.

113. The resurrection of the dead is given great prominence in the painting of the church of Tat'ev, where the men rising from their tombs fill the entire lower half of the composition. See the reproduction of one of these figures in Durnovo, *Drevnearmianskoi zhivopisi*, pl. 7.

114. Der Nersessian, *Catalogue*, p. xxxiv, pl. 54b.

115. K. Weitzmann, *Die armenische Buchmalerei des 10. und beginnenden 11. Jahrhunderts* (Bamberg, 1933), pls. I–III; Der Nersessian, *Armenia and the Byzantine Empire*, pl. XVIII.

116. Weitzmann, *Armenische Buchmalerei*, pl. IV; S. Der Nersessian, "The Date of the Initial Miniatures of the Etchmiadzin Gospel," *Art Bulletin*, 15 (1933) : 327–360, figs. 24–25, 29; B. Arak'elian, *Armenian Figured Sculpture*, figs. 16–44.

117. This stele is not mentioned by any of the previous visitors to Aght'amar but Lalayan has copied the inscription of the tombstone erected after the death of this same Catholicos, and which is dated 1346 or 1348; "Monastery of the Holy Cross," p. 210.

118. See for examples Baltrusaitis, *L'Art médiéval en Géorgie et en Arménie*, pls. XIV–XVIII, XXV.

119. *Ibid.*, pls. XXI, LXXIV, LXXVIII.

120. Bachmann, *Kirchen und Moscheen*, pl. 40.

121. Akinian, *The Catholicoses of Aght'amar*, pp. 85–107.

122. Lynch, *Armenia*, II, 133–134.

FIGURES

1   Island of Aght'amar

2 Northwest angle and west façade

3   West façade: St. Matthew

4   West façade and southwest angle

5 West façade: King Gagik and Christ, seraphim

6 West façade: seraph

7　West façade: King Gagik holding the model of the church

8   West façade: Christ

9 West façade: King Gagik

10 West façade: angel

11   West façade: arch and cross

12   West façade: cross

13   West façade: vine scroll, left half

14 West façade: vine scroll, right half

15   South façade, general view

16 South façade, left half

17 South façade: story of Jonah, Moses, angel and Christ, Virgin between Gabriel and Michael

19   South façade: Jonah and the King of Nineveh, Jonah under the gourd tree

20   South façade: Christ enthroned

21 South façade: Virgin enthroned between the Archangels Gabriel and Michael

22 South façade: sacrifice of Isaac

23   South façade: Prince Sahak, fantastic animal and eagle striking bird, King Saul, David and Goliath

24   South façade: Prince Sahak

25   South façade:
Prince Hamazasp

26 South façade: King Saul

27 South façade: David and Goliath

28 South façade: griffon, bears, and hares

30 Dome, west view

31 East façade, general view

34   East façade, central part:
Adam, St. Thaddeus,
and St. James of Nisibis

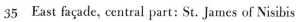

35   East façade, central part: St. James of Nisibis

36   East façade, central part: lion

37   East façade: St. John, vine scroll

38   East façade, vine scroll, left part

39   East façade: vine scroll, central section, king and attendants, Adam

40   North façade, general view

41   North façade, central section

42 North façade, left part: Samson killing a Philistine

43 North façade: Samson killing a lion

45   North façade: Isaiah

44   North façade: King Hezekiah

46   North façade, central section, lower part

48   North façade: Eve and the serpent

47   North façade: Adam and Eve

49   North façade, right half

50 North façade: St. Theodore
killing the dragon, St. Cyriacus

51 North façade:
bear eating grapes,
lion attacking a bull

52   North façade: David killing a lion

53 North façade: vine scroll

54 North façade: vine scroll

55 North façade: vine scroll

56 South door: lintel

57   Dome: creation scenes

58 Dome: creation scenes

59 South Exedra

60 Northwest view

61 Northeast view

62 East apse: Apostles Paul, Andrew, Philip

63   South exedra, left half: Annunciation, Visitation

64   West exedra, left half: Joseph's dream, flight into Egypt, Raising of Lazarus, Entry into Jerusalem

66 West exedra, pier to the right: mourning mothers

65 West exedra, right half: massacre of innocents, Christ anointed, feet washing

68   West exedra: Raising of Lazarus, Entry into Jerusalem

69 North exedra: Crucifixion, holy women and apostles at the sepulcher

70 South exedra: Second Coming of Christ

71　Cross stone of Catholicos Stephen IV, dated 1340, upper half

72　Cross stone of Catholicos Stephen IV, lower half

73 Cross stone of Catholicos Zak'aria III, dated 1444

74 Tombstone

75 Tombstone of the nineteenth century

76 Tombstone of the nineteenth century

77 Tombstones

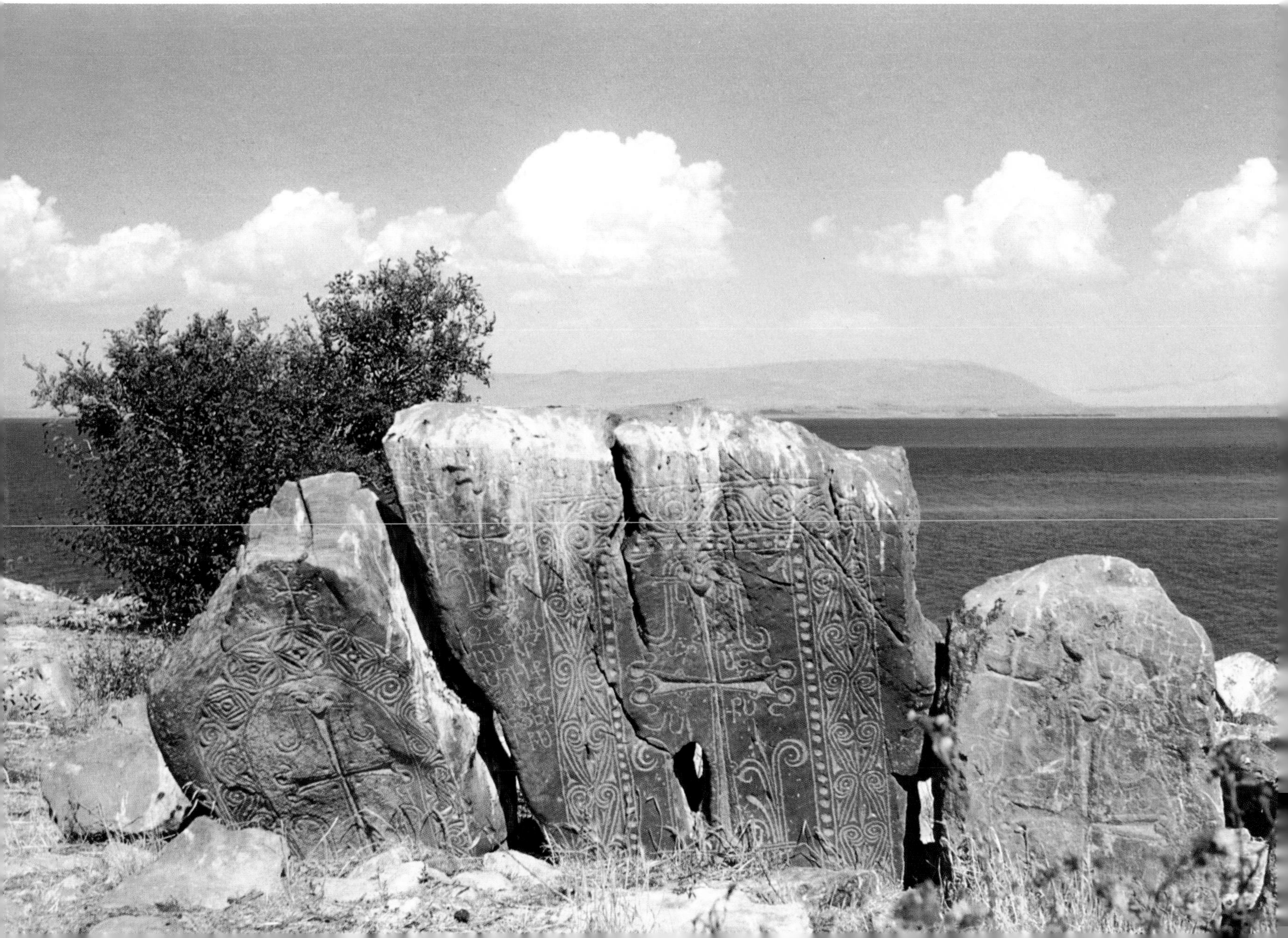